Women Leaders
in African History

For Simisola

Women Leaders
in African History

DAVID SWEETMAN

Heinemann International Literature and Textbooks
A division of Heinemann Educational Books Ltd
Halley Court, Jordan Hill, Oxford OX2 8EJ

Heinemann Educational Books Inc
361 Hanover Street, Portsmouth, New Hampshire 03801, USA

P.M.B. 5205 Ibadan · P.O. Box 45314 Nairobi
P.O. Box 61581, Marshalltown

OXFORD   LONDON   EDINBURGH
MELBOURNE   SYDNEY   AUCKLAND
SINGAPORE   TOKYO   PARIS   MADRID
BOLOGNA   IBADAN   NAIROBI
GABORONE   PORTSMOUTH (NH)

British Library Cataloguing in Publication Data

Sweetman, David
    Women leaders in African history.
    1. Women in politics—Africa
    2. Statesmen—Africa—Biography
    I. Title
    320.96′0922   DT18
    ISBN 0-435-94480-0

Set in 10/11½ pt by Oxprint Ltd, Oxford
Printed and bound in Great Britain by
Biddles Ltd, Guildford and King's Lynn

91   92   93   94   10   9   8   7   6

Contents

List of Illustrations

List of Maps

Maps drawn by Reg Piggott

Acknowledgements

The author and publishers would like to acknowledge the following sources for illustrations in this book:

Metropolitan Museum of Art, New York, Rogers Fund, 1; Peter Clayton, 2, 3, 4; P. L. Shinnie, *Meroë* (Thames and Hudson 1967), 5; R. J. Harrison-Church, 8; Stanley Gibbons Limited, 9; Trustees of the British Museum, 10, 11; Horniman Museum, London (Photo: Derrick Witty), 12; Africana Museum, Johannesburg, 16, 17; Mansell Collection, 18; Royal Geographical Society, 19, 20; Central Office of Information, 23; Capt. H. C. J. Biss, *The Relief of Kumasi* (Methuen 1901), 24; Ghana Information Service, 25; Zimbabwe National Archives, 26.

Introduction

This book brings together biographical information on the lives of twelve women leaders in African history. The aim of the book is to provide as rounded a portrait as possible of women who appear in the study of Africa's past but who in most cases have not been given the individual attention they merit.

Those chosen in no way make a definitive list of significant African women leaders. At a rough guess there are a further twenty with sufficient material for a short biography to be written. There are many other major and minor figures about whom insufficient facts are known to produce even such brief biographies as these.

The leaders in this book were chosen because they represent a geographical spread around Africa, as well as presenting chronologically the main developments in its history. Their lives were considered sufficiently different for the reader to obtain varied insights into the role of women in the continent's past. Several also appear in the general histories used in African schools, even if their importance is not fully recognized.

The first book in this series, *Black Leaders in Southern African History*, dealt with nine, mainly nineteenth-century, male personalities about whom considerable information exists. But it was not possible to give such uniform treatment to each chapter in this book.

The most unorthodox chapter, on Candace, is actually an account of the present state of our knowledge concerning the women rulers of Meroë. It was felt that it was important to include Meroë, even though no single individual stands out. The reader should bear in mind that the wealth of detail or the length of a chapter reflects the amount of information available. Queen Nzinga of Angola is of immense importance in the history of her time and region and yet we know far less about her than we do of, say, Ranavalona of Madagascar, in pan-African terms a lesser figure but of undoubted significance in her country's recent history.

Although the information for this book came from secondary sources the interpretations and opinions about the personalities are mine alone. My hope is to create interest among young people in the lives of some of Africa's outstanding female personalities and I have intentionally erred on the side of the positive.

It is helpful to remember that the most warlike and supposedly male-oriented societies sometimes had female rulers. The reason may be that if the leader is frequently away fighting he must leave his lands and possessions in charge of those he can trust, his nearest female kin. Ironically the rise of powerful male rulers often led to the establishment of a matrilineal system for, unwilling to introduce his wives' kin into the centre of power, the ruler preferred to see inheritance pass through his sister. Or again, in order to maintain his authority, the leader would take wives from each 'clan' in his group. Upon his death one of his sons would be chosen to succeed, with the boy's mother assuming a position of power as a counsellor to the new ruler.

We must, however, clear our minds of theories about matriarchal societies. Certainly many historians reveal in their writing an under-lying assumption that there was a time when women were domin-ant. Over and over again when reading about the remote history of an African people, we learn that their legendary first ancestor was a woman. And often the author will remark that this probably indi-cates that the society was matriarchal at one time. This assumption found its fullest expression in the nineteenth century when a theory known as 'The Golden Age of Matriarchy' was formulated. Accord-ing to this theory, the earliest human societies were ruled by women, but men gradually asserted themselves and 'conquered' their female counterparts. The evidence most often quoted for this theory was religious, since in many parts of the world there are myths in which a goddess, often a female fertility figure, is replaced by a god, usually a warlike male.

There is no reason to interpret these myths as records of actual events or as straightforward truthful accounts. It is more likely that such stories were meant to emphasize the fact that man had acquired a superior status *to* woman rather than implying that there had been a period of superior status *for* women. Looking at more recent times, historians have pointed out that many societies have a senior female figure as a sort of second-in-command to the head male, usually a queen-mother or royal sister and they claim that this is evidence that women have been displaced and pushed down from the leading position.

It is true that there is a remarkable similarity in the status of the queen-mother and king's-sister in many different societies across the whole of Africa. But the theory of 'The Golden Age of Matri-archy' is really only a baseless assumption, a hangover from the last century, with no concrete evidence to support it. In this century anthropologists have insisted that the theory is false and that all the evidence available indicates that since the earliest time, man has ruled. Moreover, they insist that no true matriarchal society has ever been known to exist anywhere on earth.

So by the time we enter the period of recorded history men are everywhere the dominant members of our species. Yet the interesting thing is that despite all the pressures intended to keep half the human race in subjugation, the system has proved a failure over and over again. While there may be numerically more male historical figures, those women who are remembered are frequently more extraordinary. But the heavy male bias of many historians has led to an even greater under-estimation of women and their role in our past than was true. Any history of ancient Egypt would include the name of Queen Hatshepsut, since she is too important for even the most biased historian to ignore. Yet how many people know that she was only one of several female rulers of ancient Egypt and that at one period the story of the country was dominated by a line of powerful royal women? The same is true of the history of Africa as a whole. No historian can ignore Queen Nzinga or Mmanthatisi, but again these are only two among many.

Much recently written history emphasizes social and economic factors rather than personalities. And because most of the histories of Africa are recent, African readers are consequently denied the benefit of learning about individuals with whom they can identify. Of course much of the past has been shaped by impersonal forces but it is a distortion to deny the importance of the achievements of individuals.

It would be impossible to thank the hundreds of scholars whose works I have hunted through, though the more prominent are listed in the 'Further Reading' sections at the end of each chapter. Individual thanks must be given to Dr Richard Pankhurst, Librarian of the Royal Asiatic Society and Mr David Lan for much valued advice.

David Sweetman
London, 1984

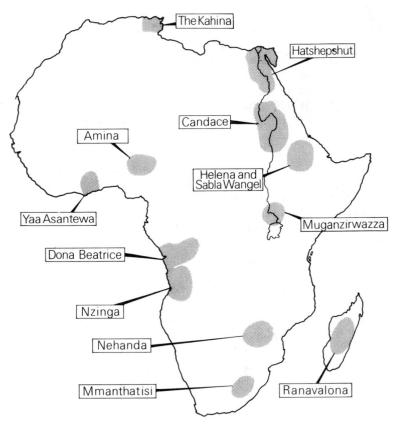

Map of Africa showing the locations of each chapter

1
Hatshepsut of Egypt

15TH CENTURY BC
RULED ABOUT 1490–68 BC

Ancient Egypt was Africa's first great civilization. It was a land of powerful kings; yet at the height of its power when its empire had spread north into the Middle East and south into Nubia, it was ruled by Queen Hatshepsut, one of the most extraordinary women in the ancient world.

The Princess Hatshepsut[1] was the daughter of the pharaoh or king of Egypt, Thutmose I. Her two elder brothers died during their father's reign and when he died, the third brother became Thutmose II in 1493 BC.[2] He married Hatshepsut to strengthen his right to the throne and they ruled jointly for eight years. But the young pharaoh died in his early thirties and his only male descendant was the six-year-old son of one of his concubines. Hatshepsut was now the single most powerful person in Egypt and although the boy was proclaimed pharaoh, as Thutmose III, she became regent and the effective ruler.

Although women in Egypt had held high positions before as regents or as strong wives of weak rulers, Hatshepsut was to become the most powerful woman to dominate the country since it had come into being. About 3,100 years before the birth of Christ, the northern and southern halves of Ancient Egypt had been united to form one country, a country that was to become Africa's first great civilization. More than a thousand years earlier groups of people had settled in the long thin valley of the Nile and planted crops in the silt left after the river flooded every year. Here they created settled communities, each worshipping different gods. They regarded their leaders as god-like, believing their powers ensured that the Nile would flood and the crops grow. Because of the richness of the land along the banks of the Nile, two or even three harvests a year were possible. This created enough wealth to support groups of priests and artists as well as the ruler, his army and his courtiers. Eventually, great rulers arose who conquered those around them until Egypt was united under one man, pharaoh, the king. Despite

1   A life-size statue of Queen Hatshepsut, from her temple at
Thebes

occasional upheavals united Egypt survived for 3,000 years with little change. The pharaoh ruled with his consort or 'great wife' and much that we know of how they lived comes from the wonderful paintings on the walls of the pyramids, the great stone tombs that were built to house the body of pharaoh and his queen to ensure that they would return to life surrounded by all the luxury that they had known in their earlier existence.

This first period of the pharaohs, called the Old Kingdom, embraced four dynasties of pharaohs. A dynasty (or line of rulers passing from father to son) would end when a pharaoh died without sons or was so weak that he was overthrown by palace intrigue. When this happened a new strong man would take power, usually reinforcing his claim by marrying one of the royal ladies of the previous dynasty. This established the importance of women as holding the right of succession. Gradually it became the custom for a new pharaoh to marry one of his sisters to further strengthen his position. Although during most of the Old Kingdom period the pharaohs were great and awesome gods too terrible even to be looked upon, by the end of the Old Kingdom the power of the pharaohs had declined: local rulers were seizing power and brief dynasties followed each other as the crisis grew. The central government was finally restored under Pharaoh Mentuhotep II sometime about 2000 BC. This was the beginning of the Middle Kingdom, as the second period of Egyptian history is called.

So successful was the country's economy during the Middle Kingdom that trade expanded outwards to the Middle East. This was to have unhappy consequences later as people from beyond the region, called Hyksos, attracted by the country's wealth, moved in and settled in the area of the Nile delta, where the great river enters the Mediterranean Sea. After nearly a hundred years of strife the Hyksos living in the delta area, joined by further waves of immigrants, rose up and established their own rule over a large part of northern (or Lower) Egypt. In unconquered Upper Egypt it was the princes of the city of Thebes who most desired to reunite Egypt. One of them, Kamose, led an uprising and nearly succeeded in driving the Hyksos out of the delta area. His successor Ahmose finally reunited the country. This event marked the beginning of the New Kingdom.

Ahmose was followed by Amenhotep I in 1546 BC and then the succession passed through the female line to a general who as Thutmose I began a new dynasty. Thutmose I and II were warrior-kings who extended their power on both their north-eastern and southern fronts. When Hatshepsut followed Thutmose II as ruler of Egypt she inherited a land whose imperial position, wealth and cultural achievements at this time made her tower above the ancient world as its most outstanding female personality.

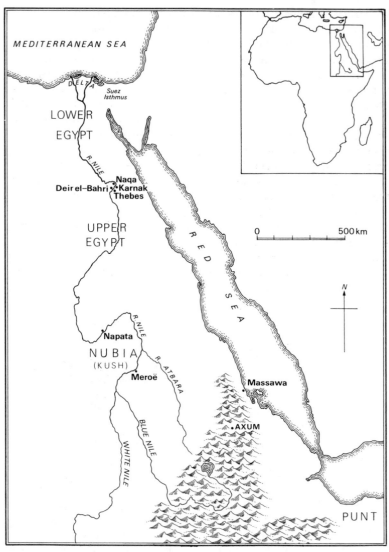

Egypt and Meroë

The first two Thutmosids had been warriors riding out in their chariots to conquer Palestine and Nubia. Under their rule Egypt was extended. Hatshepsut, on the other hand, was a builder and planner and was to bring stability and consolidation to Egypt. She surrounded herself with an outstanding group of officials, including Hapuseneb, the high priest of Amon (the principal state god of Egypt), her chancellor Nehesi and Inebny, the viceroy, or governor, of Nubia. Together they set about the development of agriculture and trade. One of the most famous events in her reign was the expedition to what the Egyptians called the land of Punt. 'Divine Punt'—the only foreign land the Egyptians did not speak of insultingly—corresponds to the coastal lands of present-day Somalia and was the source of the perfumes and incense that the Egyptians considered essential to their personal adornment and the worship of their gods. An expedition to Punt was nothing new, but whereas in the past it had been a difficult overland journey, large boats were now perfected enabling the voyage to be made by sea. These boats were probably manned by sailors from Phoenicia, a land in the Middle East then dominated by Egypt. Egypt had no tall trees so masts had to be obtained by trade with Lebanon. However, we can see from a series of murals in the temple built beside Hatshepsut's tomb that they used to lash together short lengths of wood to make seaworthy masts. The funeral temple beside her tomb at Deir el-Bahri remains one of the great architectural sites of ancient Egypt and its carved friezes tell us much about life during Hatshepsut's reign.

2 Queen Eti of Punt, relief from the temple of Queen Hatshepsut at Deir el-Bahri

Near the temple, remains have been found of myrrh trees brought from Punt to make incense, and one of the temple friezes shows her expedition being welcomed by Perehu, the chief of Punt, and Eti, his wife. The temple inscriptions record that Perehu and Eti were interested in the travellers and treated them generously. Hatshepsut also sent out mining expeditions north to Sinai for turquoise and south to Aswan for granite for her massive obelisks, the tall, square and pointed columns on which records of her achievements were carved.

At first, to strengthen her own position, she married her daughter to the young Thutmose. Then, in the second year of their joint reign, she decided to take the throne herself. From then on the little prince was no longer depicted in friezes or as her co-ruler. Increasingly she began to have herself represented as a man, wearing full pharaonic regalia, including the false beard held on by a strap that was one of the symbols of Divine Kingship. She was now referred to as 'Her Majesty the King'.

She came to rely heavily on one of her advisers, Senenmut, who was given a long string of titles and who, because little is recorded of his early life, may have risen from quite humble origins by sheer ability. It has been suggested that he was Hatshepsut's lover but that is just a guess, though it is true that at one period he was so powerful that he secretly had his image carved out of sight behind the alcove doors in the great temple at Deir el-Bahri, a presumptuous act for a mere commoner. He was certainly an energetic and able administrator and was probably responsible for carrying out the enormous building programme that Hatshepsut began in order to repair the damage caused during the struggle against the Hyksos. It has often been said that Thutmose must have hated his stepmother for stealing his throne but there is no reason to believe that as a young man he was anything but content to leave the administration of the country to her while he enjoyed himself.

At first he was sent to study at the temple of Amon. While he was there, he could have become the centre of the controversy that split the ruling group during Hatshepsut's reign. On one side were those who felt that her way was right, that Egypt's true way of life lay as it always had in the valley of the Nile and that foreign adventures were foolish. We know that the chief priest of Amon and many of the nobles thought like this. But other groups of priests thought otherwise; they wanted the vast riches that were always given to the temples after a foreign victory, booty that only a warrior-pharaoh could give them. Thutmose would have been the man this second group wanted and this may account for a curious incident at the great temple at Karnak when he was a young man. On ceremonial days the statue of Amon was brought out from its inner sanctuary and carried by white-robed priests in procession around the temple's great hall. On this occasion the statue moved away from its normal route as if searching for something. When it came to the watching Thutmose it bowed low in recognition. Of course, only the priests could have organized this deception to make clear whom they wished to see as ruler. But their protest seems to have backfired for an angry Hatshepsut had the roof of their temple removed. In this now open courtyard she set up two massive obelisks carved with stories of her greatness and coated with a glistening mixture of gold and silver.

3 Hatshepsut (centre) with the god Amon, detail from a fallen obelisk at the temple at Karnak

The young Thutmose, like his father and his grandfather, was a fighting man and we know that he spent much of his youth practising warfare and hunting. Only later would the time have come for him to claim his due. He was no doubt encouraged to do so by those, like the priests at Karnak, who hoped to benefit from his rise to power.

Hatshepsut had one disadvantage. Not having been trained as a warrior she could not lead her troops into battle nor could she risk letting anyone else do so in case they became too powerful. Consequently the outer provinces of the Egyptian empire became restless and began to break away. This strengthened Thutmose's position and there must have been a good deal of intrigue at the court. We know that Senenmut fell from favour because his inscriptions were defaced while Hatshepsut was still alive, but it took Thutmose nearly twenty years to dislodge the powerful, talented group that surrounded his stepmother. When he finally came to the throne in 1482 BC she must still have had some influence for she seems to have lived on through the early part of his reign. But how she fell from power we do not know.

Later, many of her monuments, obelisks and inscriptions were defaced and her name erased. This has been seen as a sign of the deep hatred that Thutmose III felt towards her. Yet this destruction was not total nor did it follow immediately after he came to the throne. Egyptian pharaohs often 'rewrote' history in this way. Thutmose may have wanted to replace her but must also have recognized Hatshepsut's achievements as a great ruler of a land at peace. He too was to be a great builder as well as a conqueror like his father. But much of what he achieved must be seen as a continuation of her outstanding reign, a reign in which Egypt was given peace after years of war and the opportunity to rebuild its cities and temples.

NOTES

[1] Also often given as Hashepsowe.
[2] Dates for the pharaohs are taken from *Heritage of the Pharaohs* by John Ruffle (Oxford: Phaidon, 1977).

FURTHER READING

Sir Alan Gardiner, *Egypt of the Pharaohs* (London: Oxford University Press, 1976).

Pierre Montet, *Lives of the Pharaohs* (London: Weidenfeld and Nicolson, 1968).

Cambridge Ancient History (Cambridge: Cambridge University Press, 1973).

2
Candace of Meroë

3RD CENTURY BC TO 2ND CENTURY AD
ABOUT 284 BC–AD 115[1]

Africa's second great civilization was Meroë. Whereas Egypt had few great women leaders Meroë had many, so many in fact that the outside world believed it never had a king! Despite the meagre historical evidence concerning Meroë, we know of seven of these queens by name and have some knowledge of others. An account of them and the state they ruled is one of the most fascinating stories from Africa's past.

The story begins before the reign of Queen Hatshepsut with the invasion of northern Egypt by the Hyksos, moving in from the Middle East, and their eventual conquest of the Nile delta after 2000 BC. This invasion brought about the slow decline of Egypt and weakened the country's links with Nubia, the land to the south of the Nile cataracts. But Egypt's decline did not mean the end of the Egyptian way of life in Nubia, or Kush as the Egyptians called it. (See map p. 4.)

After the pharaohs of the 18th dynasty (1554–1304 BC) had driven out the Hyksos they turned their attention to Kush. At first they occupied it as conquerors, building a massive line of defensive forts. Later, as the people became more Egyptianized, northern Kush was virtually absorbed into Egypt. Colonists were settled, creating large plantations, and Kush became a clearing house for a vast trade in gold and African produce that flowed into Egypt. The most permanent of Egypt's achievements was the establishment of the worship of the god Amon, which lasted long after they themselves had gone, for during the New Kingdom the two lands once again separated. The level of the Nile had begun to fall and by the 19th dynasty the agricultural system was destroyed, driving the colonists away. Then the collapse of authority in Egypt itself broke the final links. But though the Egyptians were gone, their religion and their traditions lived on among the Egyptianized Nubians. A new kingdom arose, based on the city of Napata, with a royal family probably descended from Hrihor, the last Egyptian viceroy before Egypt finally separated from Nubia. These Napatan kings carried on the traditions of Egypt and, most importantly, the worship of Amon.

Although there were no female rulers of Napata there were to be ruling queens of Nubia's second great capital city. To the south lay the city of Meroë and when it became the centre of the Nubian kingdom women rose to power, so much so that the outside world once believed that no man ever ruled over Meroë and that it was a land of powerful queens. By the time the Romans had occupied Egypt after the fall of Cleopatra in 30 BC, Meroë was already long known as the capital of Nubia. Much of what we know of these women of Meroë comes from Roman sources.

Candace

When the Romans began to establish themselves in Egypt they fixed their frontier at Syene near present-day Aswan. But during the rule of Governor Gaius Petronius from 25 to 21 BC many troops had to be withdrawn for a campaign in Arabia. Taking advantage of the situation and supporting local people who complained of harsh treatment at the hands of the Romans, a Kushite army attacked and overran the fort at Syene, carrying off a statue of the Roman Emperor Augustus from the market place. In 23 BC Governor Gaius

4   A Nubian princess with her entourage, from a wall painting dated about 1340 BC

Petronius returned planning vengeance. He invaded Kush and drove the Kushites beyond Napata. Then he sacked and burnt the city forcing the Kushites to beg for peace. The Roman historian Strabo who recorded these events states that the leader of the Kushites was a Queen Candace. This is a name that we find referred to elsewhere. In the Bible, the Acts of the Apostles tells of the visit of a man of Kush to Jerusalem. 'A man of great authority under Candace' (Acts 8:27). He was apparently in charge of the queen's treasury and while in Jerusalem he was converted to Christianity. Much later, in about AD 61, the Roman Emperor Nero also sent an expedition to Kush, and the writer Pliny in his *Natural History* records that the land was ruled by Queen Candace, indicating that there was a succession of queens of that name. But all these historians made the same mistake, for the word 'Candace' is a corruption of the Meroitic title 'Kdke', which was borne by all royal consorts: king's wives, queen mothers as well as ruling queens. It is believed that there were at least five ruling queens of Kush at Meroë, but as no two reigned in succession and as visitors went on recording that the country was ruled by 'Candace', even when there was a man on the throne, women may have frequently held power as they did in Egypt as chief priestess or king's sister.

In fact the little of what we know about this amazing civilization comes from outside sources or from what can be dated from buildings. The list of rulers is often intelligent guesswork and their dates estimated by such things as the length of time it might have taken for a ruler to construct his or her pyramid.

Queen Bartare

The first ruling queen, Bartare, was the third ruler to be buried at Meroë and this rise of a woman to full power, probably between 284 BC and 275 BC at the time when the move to Meroë seems to have been completed, indicates that the royal women were somehow involved in this changeover. Perhaps it was a move to weaken the authority of the priests at Napata or to emphasize a change from the Egyptian-looking north to the African south. But this is only guesswork: all we know for certain of Bartare is that she was buried in one of the three pyramids in the city's southern cemetery.

These pyramids are similar, internally, to Egyptian ones though they are smaller, more narrow and pointed. This adaptation of something originally Egyptian into something essentially Meroïtic is a feature of the city's growing culture. Regrettably, from our point of view, this spirit of change also applied to writing, and the Egyptian script which we can read was changed to Meroïtic writing which is as yet indecipherable.

Queen Shanakdakhete

The first dateable Meroïtic hieroglyphs (the picture-writing used for inscriptions) that we know of are on the tomb of the second ruling queen, Shanakdakhete, who reigned from 177 BC to 155 BC. Her inscriptions were accompanied by Egyptian hieroglyphs so we have a firmer dating for her in the list of rulers than is usual. Later still these Meroïtic hieroglyphs changed to a freer form of writing (called 'cursive') which we can read but do not understand.

Queen Amanerinas

Both queens, Bartare and Shanakdakhete, are only names to us, for until we can read Meroïtic we must rely on the second-hand reports of classical writers like Strabo. The Candace referred to by Strabo at the time of Gaius Petronius' punitive invasion was probably Queen Amanerinas[2] who may have been joint ruler with her husband Prince Akinidad, though she could have been the later Queen Amanishakete. We know that there was contact with Rome because the head from a statue of the Emperor Augustus was found when one of the palaces at Meroë was excavated. So perhaps Strabo's rather cruel description of the queen as a 'masculine sort of woman, and blind in one eye', is true. Threatened with a Roman invasion, the queen was obliged to travel to the island of Samos off the coast of Turkey to beg for peace. Meroë was inaccessible, however, and the Romans did not annex it into their empire nor demand very harsh compensation for the original attack on Syene, preferring to have the country at arm's length. The result of the destruction of Napata and the presence of an unassailable military force to the north ensured that the rulers of Meroë would look to Africa more than ever as the source of their trade and their culture.

The destruction of Napata must have been a spiritual rather than a political disaster, for the capital had already been moved to Meroë long before, during the sixth century BC. Napata remained what it had first been, a religious centre, with the great temple of Amon at Jebel Barkal across the river Nile from the city. For a long time the kings and queens of Kush continued to be buried in the old capital. But Meroë had many advantages: it is often referred to as an island because it lies in a triangle of ground surrounded on two sides by the Nile and its tributary the Atbara. As the centre of a well-watered plain it was perfect for cattle and the rulers of Kush were rich and owned vast herds.

A second reason for the move was trade. When Egypt prospered Napata was conveniently near, but later Kush was to become the centre of an Afro–Asian trade that linked eastern Africa to the Red

Sea and India; Meroë lay across that link. A third reason was iron-working for which Meroë was so important a centre that on looking at the great heaps of slag that still exist today one historian described the city as the Birmingham of Africa. One classical writer tells us that iron was so precious and the Meroites so rich that they bound common prisoners in chains of gold.

Queen Amanishakete

This change in trade would account for the fact that Queen Amanishakete, fourth in the line of queens, who ruled between 26 and 20 BC, is known to have reigned at a time of great prosperity. We know this from the amount of building that went on at the time, clear evidence of an expanding economy. Archaeologists have discovered the remains of a stone quay where the barges that sailed up and down the Nile were loaded and unloaded. We know from an engraved picture on a bronze bowl that the ordinary people lived in beehive huts made from reeds growing plentifully along the banks of the Nile, the bundles neatly and decoratively bound in ways that can still be seen in parts of Nubia today. In the engraving below we can see people milking cows and pouring the milk into bowls. But we know from other archaeological sites that the reign of Queen Amanishakete marks a change in Meroïtic society similar to that which Egypt had undergone. Originally only the kings and queens had pyramid tombs; now increased prosperity caused the rise of wealthy nobles who built tombs near to the royal pyramids hoping to be reborn with their ruler just as the Egyptians had believed. And if the Egyptian pattern was being followed then this means that there was also a middle class of scribes and doctors, artists and other skilled people. This is shown by the quality of the queen's jewellery, representing some of the best examples of Meroïtic craftsmanship.

5   Rural scene engraved on a bronze bowl from Meroë

Queen Amanitere

This golden age seems to have come to its height during the joint reign of King Natakamani and Queen Amanitere whose period, AD 25–41, coincided with part of the life of Christ. They were the greatest builders of the Meroïtic kingdom, and restored the Great

Temples of Amon both at Napata and Meroë. From their inscriptions we know that two of their children died in infancy but that a third son, Sherkarer, succeeded them.

Most interesting of all their buildings is the Lion Temple at Naqa outside Meroë, for on the walls at the entrance are carved portraits of the king and queen. They are shown in the stiff Egyptian poses of mighty rulers smiting their enemies, but Amanitere is undoubtedly African. Gone is the wasp-waisted, slim figure that the ancient Egyptians demanded of their womenfolk; here instead is the personification of that plump, wide-waisted beauty still considered most attractive in many parts of Africa today.

Apart from this temple the king and queen were responsible for much of the building at the two other principal cities in southern Nubia: Musawwarat es-Sufra and Naqa. Their buildings show a

6   Portrait of Amanitere at the entrance of the Lion Temple at Naqa

remarkable merging of Egyptian with Greek and Roman influences, all evidence of a society looking outward and able to absorb ideas from other peoples.

Otherwise Meroïtic rulers were not great temple builders, which strengthens the idea that Queen Bartare and her contemporaries moved to Meroë in order to get away from the influence and power of the priesthood at Napata.

Queen Amanikhatashan

After Natakamani and Amanitere there are no more important building activities, and the end of their joint reign marks the end of the golden age and the slow decline that brought an end to Meroë. The kingdom survived for another three hundred years, so its end was slow and peaceful—more a fading away. Trade with the outside world went on, as we know from the reign of the last queen whose name survivies, Amanikhatashan, who probably reigned from AD 83 to AD 115. Lamps imported from the Mediterranean area have survived from her reign. Two very fine ones were found in her pyramid, with handles in the form of a centaur (a mythical creature: half-man, half-horse). We also know that the connection with India was strong from the fact that the people of Meroë began to worship a completely non-Egyptian god, Apedemek, the lion deity whose three heads and several arms are Asian in origin. But although Meroë stood at the central point in a great trading empire linking Europe, Africa and Asia, it remained essentially African, drawing its ideas from Africa and feeding other ideas back into Africa. It was this situation as a crossroads of trade that may have brought about the city's end. The upheavals of the Roman Empire led to a decline in trade in the Mediterranean area while simultaneously a new power arose in Africa to the south of Meroë.

After Amanikhatashan we know of no other female rulers of Meroë except the possible existence of an unnamed queen about AD 317. She would have been the second last ruler of the city and died in AD 326. By this time the Meroïtic kingdom had almost disappeared and she must have been queen of little more than memories.

The End of Meroë

The end came after the death of this unnamed queen when the new power in eastern Africa, based on the city of Axum, in what is today Ethiopia, finally defeated the Meroites. Axum flourished at roughly the same time as Meroë. Their trade in goods between inland Africa and the East was similar, but they seem to have had few contacts until the Meroites' weakness enabled the Axumites under King Ezana to defeat them.

King Ezana's campaign against Meroë around AD 350 brought to a close one of the most glorious periods of African history. The rulers of Kush at Napata had dominated a mighty empire that had stretched from the Sudan to the Middle East; later at Meroë, their kings and queens had ruled over a prosperous and peaceful land for nearly a thousand years.

It was long believed that when the people of Meroë were driven from their city, they must have spread outwards across to West Africa and down to East Africa. It was believed that this explained why so many African kingdoms had a system of kingship similar to that of Ancient Egypt and Kush. It would also account for the spread of iron-working, a knowledge of which the Meroites had probably acquired from the Middle East. Strangely, this very reasonable theory is not supported by sufficient evidence; we have few traces of what happened to the people of Meroë. Yet it is hard to believe that so brilliant a civilization simply vanished, and we must wait for the archaeologists to discover what happened to them. The Kagiddi, a Sudanese people who live at Jebel Meidob to the west of Meroë, have a tradition that they were led to their present home by a queen. Could she have been the widow or a daughter of the king whom Ezana defeated? Did she indeed manage to lead some of her people to safety? There exists today a grave-mound said to be her tomb. Perhaps one day, when it is excavated, we may learn the truth about this fascinating legend.

NOTES

[1] The alternative Dunham list in the 'Chronology of Meroïtic rulers' in *Meroë* by P. L. Shinnie (London: Thames and Hudson, 1967) has been used because it lists more female rulers than the Hintze list.

[2] The women of Meroë named in this chapter are:

Bartare	about 284 BC–275 BC
Shanakdakhete	about 177 BC–155 BC
Amanerinas	about 99 BC–84 BC
Amanishakete	about 26 BC–20 BC
Amanitere	about AD 25–AD 41
Amanikhatashan	about AD 83–AD 115

FURTHER READING

W. Y. Adams, *Nubia, Corridor to Africa* (London: Allen Lane, 1977).

P. L. Shinnie, *Meroë* (London: Thames and Hudson, 1967).

Sir E. A. Wallis Budge, *A History of Ethiopia*, vols I and II (London: Methuen, 1928).

Bruce Trigger, *Nubia Under the Pharaohs* (London: Thames and Hudson, 1976).

3
The Kahina of the Mahgreb

ABOUT 575–702 AD

Even today the Berber peoples of North Africa set great store by prophecies that reveal the future. It is not unusual for these prophecies to be made by a woman, a prophetess believed to have supernatural powers. There are many Berber folktales of such women who have changed the course of history by predicting the outcome of a battle or the death of an enemy. Undoubtedly the most famous Berber prophetess was the Kahina who succeeded in temporarily holding back the Arab invasion of Africa in the eighth century AD.

After the death of the Prophet Mohammed in AD 632 the Moslem faith was carried by his followers into the lands that bordered Arabia and beyond. European history books tend to imagine this as a great burst of religious fanaticism, sweeping all before it and turned back only when Charles the Hammer, the king of France, defeated the Arab army at Tours in AD 732. In fact, the first real resistance that the Moslems encountered was in North Africa. Egypt was easily conquered after the Arabs had crossed the Suez isthmus in AD 640. Cyrenaica and Tripoli were overcome in the same way. But the land they called Ifriquya (by which they meant what is today Tunisia) was to prove more difficult. This was Byzantine Africa, the last remnant of the great Roman African Empire. The empire was now ruled from the east, from Byzantium, which later became Christian Constantinople, then Turkish Istanbul. The history of North Africa in classical times is in one way the story of the relationship of the native people, the Berbers, with those from outside who wished to impose their rule on the land.

Recognizing the Arab threat the Byzantine governor, Gregory, first tried to get the support of the Berbers. Without them resistance would have been impossible. But at the first battle in AD 647 the Byzantine army was defeated and Gregory was killed. Arab legend has embellished their victory with marvellous exploits, such as the story of Gregory's daughter Yamina who is said to have fought like a she-devil, riding into the heart of the battle protected from the burning sun by a parasol of peacock feathers. After her capture she escaped slavery by leaping from her camel and breaking her neck.

Yet despite such a woman, Byzantine resistance had been proved weak. It was not the foreigners who were to halt the Arab advance but the Berbers themselves. Again it was to be a woman who would lead them. Like Yamina, she was a woman whose life is known mainly from legends.

The Arabs had come for gold and having seized what they could carry they retreated to the safety of Egypt. But they had seen the weakness of their enemy and it was only a matter of time before they would return.

The first great Berber resistance leader, Kosaila, defeated and killed the leader of the next Arab invasion, Oqbah Ibn Nafi[1], in 683. The Berbers occupied the holy city of Kairouan, which had been founded by Oqbah. But in 686, after a fierce battle, Kosaila was killed, though the combined Berber and Byzantine force was again able to hold back the main Arab advance.

The centre of resistance now passed from the plains of Tunisia to the stronghold of the Aurès mountains, to a Berber group, the Jerawa, ruled over by a woman who was at last to make the invaders doubt that they would win. She is known to us by a given name, the Kahina, which is variously translated as 'prophetess' or 'sorcerer'. The Arab historian Ibn Khaldun (1332–1406) says that her name was Dihya, but there is a Berber group with a similar name and she may have been associated with them and their name confused with hers. She may not have been of straightforward Berber descent. Some sources name her father Matiya (Mathias) which would make her of

7   Berber women from the Aurès Mountains. The Kahina may have looked much like this

mixed Byzantine and Berber blood, a fact which if true could explain the ease with which she was able to unite the resistance to the outsiders. Furthermore, she is said to have had two sons, one by a Greek father and the other by a Berber, which would have further strengthened her position as leader of the two groups.

The reason for her resistance was long thought to be religious. Many Berber groups had adopted the Jewish faith, which they had acquired from groups of Jews who had settled in North Africa after the destruction of their homeland in AD 638. As a Jew the Kahina would have opposed the Moslem advance. It now seems likely, however, that the Jerawa, like other Berber groups, had been converted to Christianity before the spread of Islam. As a Christian, the Kahina would have been no more welcoming to the Moslems than if she were a Jew, but in fact religion was only one reason for her opposition. The Arabs were seen as destroyers, rootless warriors pillaging settled communities or destroying established agricultural systems. To the Kahina they were barbarians and had to be opposed. Only later, with the establishment of their empire, were the Arabs to create their admirable civilization.

The role of the resistance leader can have been no easy task for the Kahina. At the time of Kosaila's death she was a widow and already very old, though just how old we do not know. Legend says that she lived to be 127 and was queen of the Aurès for thirty-five years. This is probably exaggerated but she may indeed have lived to a great age. Equally dramatic is the reason for the nickname that the Arabs gave her, the sorceress, for she was a prophetess of a kind that exists in North Africa to this day. Such a prophetess goes into a trance, often with the aid of music and drumming. She may spin, round and round, with her hair streaming out, beating her breasts until at the height of her trance she speaks, telling her listeners what will happen in the future, pouring out knowledge from sources closed to ordinary mortals until in the end she falls to the ground, exhausted and barely conscious. The power of prophecy would have given the Kahina great authority over her people.

The next Arab invasion was led by Hassan ibn al-Nu'man al-Ghassani who decided to divide his opponents by first removing the Byzantine resistance. He took Carthage in 695 which, although later retaken by a relief fleet, was seen as a deadly blow to the Byzantine spirit. He next turned his attention to the Aurès mountains, the stronghold of Berber resistance. The Kahina first destroyed Baghaya, her own capital, so that it could not fall into enemy hands. The two armies met on the banks of the river Meskiana in a battle that was so disastrous for Hassan that the Arabs named the *oued* (river) near where it occurred 'the river of trials'. A further defeat near the Tunisian town of Gabès finally crushed Hassan's forces and they were driven back into Tripolitania.

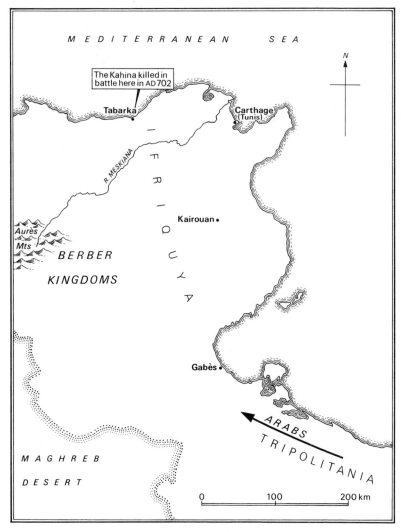

Byzantine Africa at the time of the Kahina

Three years later Hassan was able to retake Carthage. Byzantine strength was exhausted, the remnants of their forces scattered west along the coast or to the Balearic Islands. He founded the city of Tunis close to Carthage and waited: he realized that the Kahina would now not be so easy to defeat.

In fact, her eventual downfall seems to have been largely her own fault. For five years she ruled her new Berber kingdom, but the qualities that had made her a good resistance leader were not those of a ruler. She was certainly a just and merciful monarch as even her enemies were prepared to testify, for she even adopted an Arab prisoner, a move that some have interpreted as a sign that she wished to come to terms with the invaders, to work out some way in which they could all live together. But Hassan's every action made it clear that he was only waiting to attack. In desperation the Kahina embarked on the policy that was to bring about her downfall. To prevent the Arabs from living off the land, she adopted a scorched-earth policy, burning trees and destroying crops and towns. The extent of this destruction has been exaggerated but the results were sadly obvious. The settled farming Berbers, their livelihood destroyed by her tactics, withdrew from the alliance. In fact many now begged Hassan to intervene to protect them.

Having received reinforcements from the caliph, Hassan invaded, probably in 697 or 698. It took him another four years to track down his enemy. The Berbers were divided and in the Aurès mountains the Kahina's prophecies grew wild with messages of destruction. It was one of these prophecies that enabled her to foretell her own defeat and so warn her two sons to change sides on the eve of the battle. Fought near Gabès in 701, this battle was indeed a defeat. The Kahina was, however, able to escape and flee back to the mountains, pursued by Hassan. A final battle was fought near Tabarka, where she was killed near a well which was long called the Bir el-Kahina. Her head was sent to the caliph and Berber resistance came to an end.

Yet, as before, the Berbers would gradually come to dominate their conquerors. It was a Berber Moslem, Tariq Ibn Ziyad, who first carried Islam to Spain; naming the rock where he landed Jebel al-Tariq, which is today's Gibralter. The great civilization of Moslem Spain was as much a product of Berber efforts as Arab ingenuity. But it was undoubtedly the Kahina who most inspired the Berbers long after their absorption into the Islamic empire.

NOTES

[1] The rendering of Arabic names is confused by the differences between English and French transcription. Unless a more familiar form has become established, the English transcription has been used. African forms of Arabic names are used where appropriate.

FURTHER READING

Susan Raven, *Rome in Africa* (London: Evans, 1969).
Charles-André Julien, *History of North Africa* (London: Routledge and Kegan Paul, 1970).
E. W. Bovill, *The Golden Trade of the Moors* (London: Oxford University Press, 1958).

4
Amina of Hausaland
15TH OR 16TH CENTURY

The Hausa men of West Africa are proud and independent, yet their most famous ruler and greatest warrior was a woman, Queen Amina.

She is said to have created the only Hausa empire and to have led into battle a fierce army of horsemen. Indeed, so powerful is the memory of her exploits that songs of her deeds are still sung today.

By the end of the eighth century AD Arab explorers were aware of a great civilization to the south of the Sahara. This was ancient Ghana, situated in an area further west than present-day Ghana. The beginning of ancient Ghana's power roughly coincides with the spread of Islam in North Africa. From that time, over the next 1,500 years, the great states of the western Sudan rose, flourished and fell, each passing on to the next the mantle of power, each state centred a little further east—Ghana, Mali, Songhay, Kanem Bornu, Sokoto. In the midst of these, the seven states that make up Hausaland came into being around AD 1050. Before the separate Hausa states were established, this area of West Africa was ruled by a dynasty of queens—seventeen in all. Later Islamic scholars, using older Arabic stories mixed with local tales, created a legend to explain the sudden development of the Hausa peoples: Shawata, the last of the seventeen queens, offers marriage to any man who will slay Sarki, a monstrous snake that lives in the well of the town of Daura. Abyazidu (also known as Bayajida), a prince of Baghdad, comes to Hausaland by way of Bornu, slays Sarki and marries the queen. It is their son Bawo who is held to be the founding father of the original seven Hausa states: Daura, Kano, Zazzau, Gobir, Katsina, Rano and Garun Gabas. They form an area of some 500 square kilometres, the core of Hausaland.

As the populations of these states increased so they grew wealthy and attracted the attention of other powers. Yet the Hausa are a tough people and the only explanation why for much of their history they were under outside domination must lie in the fact that they

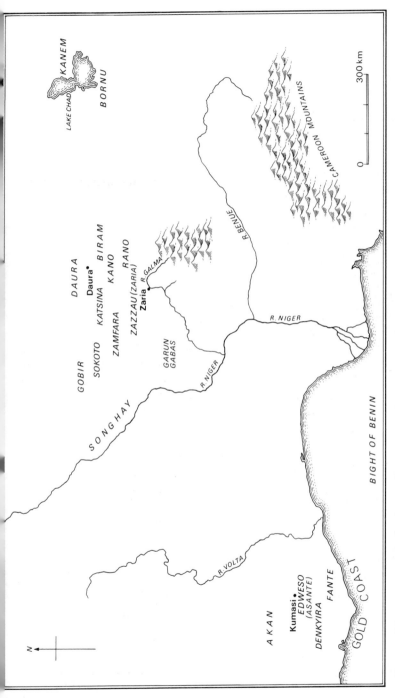

Centre: Hausa states at the time of Amina's rule. Left: the Asante kingdom (see Chapter 11)

were split into these seven separate states. Only two Hausa leaders were conquerors and the first of these was a woman, queen Amina of Zazzau who succeeded in extending the boundaries of Hausaland outside its original core.

Legend or truth?

There are many legends about Amina as she is usually known, though her full name was Aminatu. The tales of her exploits have made her one of the most famous African women, second only to Nzinga of Angola. Because much of the early written material about her is contradictory, some historians cautiously believe that she may be just a legend. However, despite the contradictions, she is mentioned in three of the four main sources for the history of the Hausa. The *Abuja Chronicle*[1] and *Infaku'l Maisuri* of Sultan Muhammadu Bello[2] both describe her as a daughter of the ruling house but not as a ruler in her own right and the traditional list of Hausa rulers contained in the *Labarun Hausawa da Makwabtansu* does not mention her at all.[3] This need not surprise us: Moslem chroniclers often left out women rulers or lessened the significance of their actions. But the Kano Chronicle[4] describes her as a ruler who flourished in the early fifteenth century. The majority voice is that she did exist though exactly when is much harder to decide.

Zazzau

The eighteenth ruler of Zazzau, according to the *Zaria Chronicle*, introduced Islam in the late fifteenth or early sixteenth century. The twentieth king, Nohir, had no sons and on his death in 1535 his brother inherited his throne. When he too had died within the year the choice of ruler fell on Nohir's daughter, Bakwa Turunku.

The people of Zazzau had had several capital towns and this queen seems to have continued the tradition. First she had her slaves build the town of Turunku while she was away fighting the Nupe; then, when it became obvious that the new town would outgrow its water supply, she built a stronghold further to the north commanding the river Galma. This new capital she named after her younger daughter Zaria, a name which thereupon replaced Zazzau as the name of the state itself. But it was her elder daughter Amina who inherited Bakwa Turunku's warlike spirit.

Amina was sixteen when her mother became queen and she was given the traditional title of *magajiya*. Despite presents of slaves and expensive clothes sent by suitors who hoped to marry her she refused them all. She was too independent to be tied to one man.

8 The old walls of Zaria, an example of the fortifications often known as 'Amina's walls'

Here the record varies. By one account she became queen sometime around 1536 and reigned until 1573; by another account, Karama became king, and because of her dashing military exploits during his reign Amina became queen on his death in 1576. She then began the conquest of the other Hausa states that has made her so famous. According to the Sultan Muhammadu Bello of Sokoto, she 'made war upon these countries and overcame them entirely so that the people of Katsina paid tribute to her and the men of Kano. She also made war on the cities of Bauchi till her kingdom reached to the sea in the south and the west.' Soon other rulers sent gifts. The ruler of Nupe sent forty eunuchs and 10,000 kola nuts. Tradition credits her with being the first to have such luxuries in Hausaland. No matter which dates they give for her, the different sources all credit her with conquests stretching over thirty-four years. Whether she ever married is disputed, but she is said to have taken a new lover in every town she conquered. Since she always left the following day the unfortunate man was beheaded in the morning. She is said to have built a great many walled encampments on her various campaigns and many surviving fortifications bear her name. However, this is one reason for questioning her legend, since many of these walls may date back to the twelfth century.

Hausa traders

If we can place Amina in the fifteenth or sixteenth centuries, then her reign coincides with a period of expansion in Hausa trade. The goods produced by the Hausa craftsmen—smiths, weavers, dyers, tanners and leather-workers—were greatly in demand outside their own borders. Hausa centres became market towns, and the Hausa language was used by traders in much of the western Sudan. During Amina's reign Zaria became the centre of the north–south Saharan trade and the east–west Sudan trade.

9 The legend of Amina riding at the head of her troops is celebrated in this special issue Nigerian stamp

Amina died in Atagara, a town in one of her southern conquests. The legend of their warrior-queen riding out at the head of her thousand horsemen has lived on among the Hausa. A song in her honour says: 'Amina daughter of Nikatau, a woman as capable as a man'.

Gradually the power of Zaria declined and in 1734 it was conquered by Bornu. But if her military achievements were lost the expansion of trade during her reign was to outlive them. No matter who their nominal rulers were, the Hausa remained independent manufacturers and travelling pedlars of their goods. As the *Kano Chronicle* says of Amina: 'In her time the whole products of the west were brought to Hausaland.'[5]

NOTES
[1] Mallam Hassan and Mallam Shu'aibu, *A Chronicle of Abuja*, trans. F. Heath (Ibadan, 1952).
[2] Sultan Muhammadu Bello, *Infaku'l Maisuri*, trans. E. J. Arnett in *The Rise of the Sokoto Fulani* (Kano, 1922).
[3] *Labarun Hausawa da Makwabtansu*, 2 vols (Zaria: Translation Bureau, 1932 and 1933).
[4] *Kano Chronicle*, quoted in H. R. Palmer, *Sudanese Memoirs*, vol III (Lagos, 1928)
[5] Ibid., p. 109.

FURTHER READING
John Hatch, *Nigeria* (London: Secker and Warburg, 1971).
Michael Crowder, *The Story of Nigeria* (London: Faber and Faber, 1962).
S. J. Hogben and A. H. M. Kirk-Greene, *The Emirates of Northern Nigeria* (London: Oxford University Press, 1966).

5
Helena and Sabla Wangel of Ethiopia

16TH CENTURY
HELENA d.1522; SABLA WANGEL d.1568

The sixteenth century was a time of crisis in Ethiopian history;
that the country survived near destruction was due to the
resourcefulness and courage of the Empress Helena and her
successor Sabla Wangel.

Sometime about a thousand years ago many Europeans came to
believe that in the little-known regions beyond the Middle East
there existed a wondrous Christian realm ruled over by a priest-king
or 'prester' called John. At first this land was believed by some to be
in Asia but when vague news of Christian Ethiopia filtered through
to the west, the land of Prester John was eventually assumed to lie
south of Egypt. By the fifteenth century it was believed that Prester
John ruled over forty-two minor kings, that he was surrounded by
fantastic animals, some of them half-men, half-horse, often breathing fire, and that his palace was made of crystal and gems where
even his vast table was a solid emerald set on pillars of amethyst. But
most important of all was the fact that he was a Christian prince and
that his servants were archbishops and other priests. In the midst of
all this Prester John was a simple, holy man, never turning away the
needy from his presence. And, fortunately for Europe, he was the
arch-enemy of Islam.(For picture, see p. 30.)

So it was that in the fifteenth and sixteenth centuries, Europeans
believed that Ethiopia was not only ruled by a man, but by a priest in
a land of priests in which women would hardly play a great part. It
must, therefore, have surprised the first European to make his way
to the Ethiopian court that the only person of any importance who
recognized his significance was a woman, the Empress Helena.[1]

The Empress Helena

Ethiopia was separated from contact with other Christian lands by its surrounding Moslem neighbours. The Ethiopian empire itself contained Moslem states within its shifting borders and this, as well as frequent rebellions by the *rases* (provincial lords), meant that the emperor was constantly forced to move about the country to keep rebellious provinces under control. The court lived in royal camps, virtually a movable city of tents with a special tented enclosure for the empress and her ladies. The only permanent places in the country were the great monasteries, so they alone could act as patrons of art and architecture.

The emperor was a figure held in great awe, hidden from ordinary people behind brocade curtains in his vast scarlet tent, or protected behind veils held by his nearest courtiers as he rode out, preceded by chained lions, the symbols of his authority. The ancient practice of imprisoning his royal brothers in mountain-top fortresses was revived. The emperor's rule was absolute: he was the *negus nagast* (the king of kings), but only so long as he suppressed any hint of revolt among the warlike peoples and clans that made up his country. When all was well the Ethiopians came down from the mountains and occupied the surrounding lands; otherwise they retreated to safety.

That this isolation was not to last was due to two factors: the adventurous Portuguese sailors who were exploring every corner of the globe where their sailing ships could take them, and the rise of the Ottoman rulers of Turkey who were making themselves masters of the Islamic world, reviving Moslem ideas of the *jihad* (holy war) against unbelievers. Such a religious revival was bound to affect Ethiopia's relations with its neighbouring independent Moslem states, the lands that make up present-day eastern Ethiopia. It had been the policy of some emperors to enter into diplomatic marriages with Moslem princesses in order to make friends of these border states. The fact that this obliged them to commit polygamy was excused on the grounds that their wives were subsequently converted to Christianity. The Emperor Baeda Maryam had married the daughter of the Moslem king of Doaro. On baptism she took the name of Helena. Far from being the usual passive consort, Helena was an intelligent far-seeing woman who, perhaps because of her knowledge of the Moslem world from which she came, was able to anticipate the disaster that was about to overwhelm her adopted country. She was also aware of another power. In 1498 Vasco da Gama, the Portuguese explorer, had entered the Indian Ocean. Helena had heard of the Portuguese landings on the coast and knew that the visitors were Christians. She guessed that they might be useful as enemies of Islam.

10   Prester John, from a sixteenth-century atlas

It was this foresight and shrewdness that made her one of the most outstanding women in Ethiopian history. She was effectively to dominate the policies of the country during the four reigns after her husband's death.

When Baeda Maryam died in 1478 Helena became regent for their son Iskander, who was also known as Constantine. It is probable that these names are a reference to the Constantine who was the first

Christian Emperor of Byzantium in the fourth century AD. It was he who had written to Ezana, the first Christian ruler of Axum, the city-state that preceded Ethiopia. And it was the Emperor Constantine's mother, Saint Helena, who was believed by many to have discovered the True Cross. During the reign of the Ethiopian Emperor Dawit I (1380–1412), what was believed to be wood from the cross had been brought from Jerusalem and two small crucifixes made from it. It was in celebration of this event that Dawit had decreed that the priests of Ethiopia should replace their previously plain robes for ones embroidered with 'Maskal daisies', a yellow flower in bloom during the season of the festival.

The Empress Helena of Ethiopia was not just a nominal convert to Christianity. She is remembered as a good and holy person, proof of which can be found in the two religious books that she wrote, *Praise Ye with Organs* and *Rays of the Sun*. Her entire life was dedicated to protecting her adopted country from being overrun by those who followed her former religion of Islam.

During Iskander's minority Helena rebuilt many of the religious buildings, churches and monasteries that had been destroyed in the frequent wars between Christians and Moslems. When Iskander came of age and ruled in his own right he was constantly occupied with repelling attacks launched by the sultan of Adal. This may explain why only Helena was able to realize the importance of the arrival in Ethiopia of one of the Portuguese adventurers, Pedro de Covilham.

De Covilham had been sent by King John II of Portugal to find Prester John and to enlist his aid against the rising tide of the Moslem religious revival. The court of the Emperor Iskander can hardly have been what de Covilham expected to find at the end of the difficult journey up to the highland kingdom. It is probable that he was forbidden to leave, for he remained in Ethiopia for the rest of his life. If his hopes of enlisting the magnificent resources of Prester John had been dashed, his presence was to raise the opposite hope in the mind of the Empress Helena, since she quickly realized that de Covilham represented a powerful and adventurous Christian kingdom. She was also shrewd enough to realize that the Portuguese wanted access to the spice-producing regions of the Far East and therefore needed control of the Indian Ocean trade routes then dominated by the Moslem Arabs. The destruction of the Moslem states on the Red Sea coast would therefore help both Portugal and Ethiopia.

Iskander was killed fighting the sultan of Adal and she acted as regent for his child. But the boy, Amda Sion II, died after a few months and Helena's second son, Naod, became *negus* in 1494. He wisely allowed himself to be guided by his mother who was setting up a series of protective alliances with those Moslem states, such as

Egypt, who were trying to stop the Ottoman Turks dominating the Islamic world. But fourteen years later in 1508 Naod was dead and Helena was again regent, this time for his son, the twelve-year-old Lebna Dengel.

It was during this regency that the two most powerful external forces, Portugal and Turkey, began to intrude increasingly on Ethiopian affairs.

The Portuguese gained control of the Red Sea and the East African coastal waters, driving out the Egyptian and Indian fleets. But the Turks conquered Egypt in 1517 and soon replaced the Arabs in the Indian Ocean. Their presence was a tremendous stimulus to Ethiopia's traditional Moslem enemies.

These upheavals left Helena with no choice: she had to seek the aid of the only other power available. In the first year of her last regency, 1508, two further Portuguese envoys had arrived with letters from Manuel, the new king of Portugal, to Prester John. Dom Manuel was seeking the Prester's aid in his struggle against Egypt for control of the Red Sea. Helena decided that the time was right to end Ethiopia's isolation, not least to get help in the seemingly never-ending struggle against the sultanate of Adal. So in 1509 she sent a messenger, Mathew, with a letter to the Portuguese king. This letter to 'our very dear and well-loved brother' proposed an alliance of the two Christian states against the Turks. 'In such a cause', the empress wrote, 'I would not spare myself.' She explained that Ethiopia had no sea forces but that her armies allied to Portugal's navy would overcome their enemies: 'We need conjunction and alliance with you, who are so powerful in warfare on the sea.' To reinforce the sincerity of her appeal she sent the king magnificent gifts: perhaps the most touching and, to the Ethiopians, the most splendid were two tiny crucifixes said to have come from the wood of the True Cross on which Christ died in Jerusalem.

That this gracious gift and eloquent letter should have had so little effect is one of the saddest disappointments in Ethiopia's history— the journey to Portugal was long and difficult, and in the time it took conditions changed. The king of Portugal had wanted an alliance with the magical realm of Prester John and he was far from impressed with reports of the harassed land of the Empress Helena.

Eleven years passed before Mathew was able to return, accompanied by a Portuguese group led by Rodrigo da Lima but without the treaty of alliance that Helena had hoped for. In any case, during the intervening period the situation in Ethiopia had also changed. Lebna Dengel had come of age and assumed power. Though still an important adviser, Helena was no longer in direct control of events. For the remaining years of her life she could only try to stop him from making hasty and sometimes foolish decisions. By the time she died in 1522 her warnings of the Moslem threat had been forgotten.

11   Lady escorted by spearmen, from an Ethiopian manuscript

Disaster

At first there seemed to be some reason for assuming that the danger
had passed. Lebna Dengel was a competent soldier and in 1517 he
succeeded in conquering Adal—the last of the Moslem states within
the Ethiopian empire to continue the struggle to recover its independence. This victory gave Lebna Dengel a false sense of security. He
made little attempt to gain any advantage from the latest Portuguese
mission other than to agree that they should occupy the Red Sea
ports, particularly Massawa, that he knew were threatened by the
Turks. Lebna Dengel had little understanding of the Moslem states
and lacked tact in his handling of them. The Moslem king of Hadya
sent his daughter as a wife for him, but he refused to marry her
because she had projecting front teeth. The girl had, however, been
baptized a Christian and could not return to her family. Lebna
Dengel solved the problem by marrying her to one of his nobles, an
insult that her father never forgave.

But worse than this lack of tact and foresight was Lebna Dengel's temperament which, after Helena's death, was seldom checked. He frequently dismissed high officials and used degrading punishments against the nobles, which made him unpopular with the very people whose support he needed. But it was his own overconfidence that led to his downfall.

The recent upheavals had virtually halted commerce in the Red Sea area and had caused considerable hardship in the coastal region. Inevitably, it was in Moslem Adal where resentment most quickly produced revolution. A young agitator, Ahmed Ibn Ibrahim, nicknamed Gran (the left-handed), deposed the sultan of Adal and, taking the religious title of *imam*, proceeded on a holy war against Ethiopia. Foolishly underestimating his enemy, Lebna Dengel engaged him with only half the Ethiopian army and was crushingly defeated at the battle of Shembera Kure in 1529. Ahmed Gran then embarked upon a reign of terror and destruction. So many churches and monasteries, including the rebuilt cathedral of Axum, were destroyed that Ethiopia's cultural heritage was almost annihilated. The majority of the population was forced to become Moslems and the army was dispersed. Most of the royal family were killed or captured and Lebna Dengel became a fugitive constantly in fear of Ahmed Gran's troops. Finally and tragically the wisdom of the Empress Helena was made apparent and a desperate mission was sent begging the Portuguese king to come to the aid of his Christian brother.

By 1539 the harassed and exhausted Lebna Dengel had only one refuge left, the monastery on the flat mountain top at Debra Damo, which could be reached only by a basket-lift hauled up from the top.

By now Lebna Dengel was dying, a lonely and bankrupt man who had lost an empire. He was to learn too late that John III of Portugal had ordered his viceroy in Goa on the west coast of India to send help. Lebna Dengel died in September 1540 leaving all that remained of his realm—the top of an isolated mountain—in the charge of his widow, the Empress Sabla Wangel.

Rescue

In 1539 a small Portuguese force of four hundred men was put ashore near Massawa. It was led by a dashing young officer, Christopher da Gama, son of the explorer Vasco da Gama. To the young man and his high-spirited soldiers the whole enterprise seemed like a great adventure, with themselves as knights-errant or crusaders come to save a beleaguered Christian outpost. This air of unreality was soon dispelled when a hundred of the men disobeyed orders and set off impetuously for the interior, only to be ambushed and slaughtered by Ahmed Gran's men.

Da Gama now realized that he was helplessly outnumbered and could certainly not defeat Gran. The most he could do would be to give hope to the surviving Ethiopians to encourage them to rally their scattered forces. The young captain realized that the most important person in the country was the queen mother, Sabla Wangel, and he consequently set off on the difficult journey up the escarpment and across the highlands to Debra Damo.

The queen mother had known nothing but sadness. She had not only lost her husband but had also seen her eldest son, Fiqtor, killed and her fourth son, Minas, taken prisoner. Her second son Claudius, the new emperor, was suffering the same harassment as his father, moving from place to place, desperately trying to gather soldiers while only just evading the Moslem troops sent to track him down.

That Sabla Wangel was still considered to be an important woman was shown by the attempts made to capture her; only the isolation of Debra Damo protected her from the attack and siege laid by Gran's ally, the king of Zeila. As the Portuguese chronicler said: 'It appeared constructed by the hands of God to preserve this lady and her following from captivity . . . . For the King of Zeila came against it . . . to get the Queen, whom he much desired into his hands, as she is very beautiful.'[2]

And that was just what the young Christopher da Gama discovered when the queen was lowered down from the monastery to inspect his troops. All the feelings of high romance must have returned for a moment—the beautiful, tragic queen veiled in black silk embroidered with flowers, saluted by her rescuer, the gallant young captain, a cloak over his shoulders, his black cap in his hand. But it was only a moment's pause in a continuing nightmare. The queen mother had realized that this small troop of Portuguese soldiers was her country's only hope. Her presence might rally the Ethiopians to them. If they could join forces with Claudius it might just be possible to confront Ahmed Gran. It must have seemed like a desperate gamble as they set off, the queen and her ladies surrounded by her Portuguese bodyguard at the rear of the narrow column making its way across the difficult mountain passes.

Happily, the presence of the queen had the desired effect of bringing the people out of hiding, either as volunteers for their army or with gifts of food and other provisions. But their numbers were still pitifully low when in February 1542 they came upon another mountain fortress, this time occupied by the Moslems. They were obliged to storm it, with the loss of eight dead and forty wounded. Sabla Wangel and her ladies won the devotion of the soldiers by moving among the men, helping the hurt and comforting the dying.

Worse than the number of dead and wounded was the fact that Ahmed Gran was now alerted to the Portuguese advance. He at once recalled his forces from their pursuit of Claudius and gathered them, nearly 20,000-strong, for a pitched battle against the queen mother and her young allies.

The two armies met in a natural amphitheatre set amidst a circle of low hills. On one side was the beautiful queen and her ladies, surrounded by her knights, while on the other was an almost identical scene—for Ahmed Gran's wife, Bati Del Wanbara, another formidable woman, had insisted on accompanying her husband on his campaign. Despite the grumbles of the soldiers who were obliged to carry her and her baggage across the difficult mountain passes she had travelled throughout the invasion, halting only to give birth to her two sons, Muhammad and Ahmad.

The subsequent battle was predictably a disaster for the heavily outnumbered Portuguese who were quickly surrounded and cut to pieces by Gran's cavalry. When nightfall came da Gama decided on a desperate gamble to save the queen, attempting to break out of his encirclement with a rapid charge. Quietly the baggage and the cannon were loaded and the column marched forward, straight at the centre of the Moslem army. It ought not to have succeeded, but in the confusion that followed so unexpected a move Ahmed Gran was unhorsed and wounded and as he was carried away his troops broke ranks, letting the Portuguese through. It was a lucky escape but hardly a victory when over a quarter of the surviving Portuguese were wounded, including da Gama himself. But at least they had earned a year's breathing space.

Gran, however, was now determined to wipe out the Ethiopians. Sabla Wangel's captured son, Minas, was sent as a gift to the Turkish pasha of the Red Sea port of Zabid and he in return sent Turkish reinforcements. On the Ethiopian side, Claudius had at last managed to raise some troops but before the two Christian armies could join up, Gran's new forces came upon the Portuguese and utterly defeated them. Again covered by a desperate charge, a group managed to escape with the queen mother, leaving behind their young captain badly wounded. He might have escaped detection had it not been for what the Ethiopians believed was the devil disguised as an old woman, who led the Moslems to him. Gran had da Gama horribly tortured before killing him, but it was now the turn of the Moslem leader to make a serious mistake. Confident that he had put an end to the Portuguese menace he allowed the Turkish troops to return to Zabid just as the remnants of the Portuguese force, along with the queen mother, joined up with Claudius's army. It was now the Ethiopians who swept down upon their enemies and scattered them, killing the hated Gran and capturing his son Muhammad.

12 The death of Christopher da Gama (above) and the fall of Ahmed Gran (below), from a twentieth-century Ethiopian painting

Del Wanbara

Sabla Wangel's joy was Bati Del Wanbara's sorrow. She was determined to avenge her husband and punish the Christians. At first she was forced to flee north to the region of the river Atbara, a tributary of the Nile, but eventually she made her way to the city of Harar, which had become the centre of Moslem resistance.

Her first task brought her for a moment close to the woman who had been her enemy. It had been Del Wanbara's intervention that had originally saved the life of Prince Minas; now an exchange was arranged so that her own son Muhammad could return to her. But this done, she set about trying to find a successor for Gran.

She settled on his nephew, Nur Ibn Mujahid, whom she married and then sent with a new Moslem army against her hated enemies. This attack launched in 1559 led to the death of Claudius, but the Ethiopians had been building up their strength and continued the struggle for twelve years, led by the new Emperor Minas. Neither side won and both were eventually to stop fighting because of the arrival of a common enemy—the Galla.

The Galla

The Galla tribes, who are known today as the Oromo, are the largest of the Kushite peoples in the south. First they migrated along the coastal areas and then, while the Christian Ethiopians were pre-occupied with their wars, slowly advanced into the highland regions. Realizing that Harar was at risk Nur Ibn Mujahid decided to stop the fighting, finally ending the threat of a Moslem occupation of the Ethiopian empire. Minas had died after only four years as emperor and it was Sabla Wangel's influence that assured the throne for her grandson, Sarsa Dengel. Although he was one of Ethiopia's greatest soldiers there was little he could do but try to hold back the insistent Galla advance, a problem that was to preoccupy his successors for the next three centuries. Equally tragic was the loss of Massawa and the other coastal ports to the Turks, a loss that again isolated the highlands both commercially and culturally.

This might have been counterbalanced by the presence of the surviving Portuguese soldiers, many of whom had decided to stay. For a time they influenced many aspects of Ethiopian life, particularly architecture, but there was one deep-seated problem—the Portuguese insistence that the Coptic Church be replaced by the Roman Catholic faith. Sabla Wangel was foremost in defending the Ethiopian church and eventually European influence dwindled.

Despite the disadvantages of isolation, Ethiopia was able to remain an independent state into the present century. That this proved possible was largely due to the foresight and courage of her two outstanding 'guardians', Helena and Sabla Wangel.

NOTES

[1] In general, names and dates are taken from the *Dictionary of African Biography* of the *Encyclopedia Africana* as this has been produced under the auspices of the Organization of African Unity and can be seen as providing standardization acceptable to African scholars. Where there are better-known alternative names these have been kept as their replacement would confuse the general reader. Other names and dates conform to the *Dictionary of Ethiopian Biography*, vol. 1 (Addis Ababa: Institute of Ethiopian Studies, 1975). Where possible, diacritical marks have been removed as these are confusing to the non-specialist. The few names and dates not included in these two excellent works are taken from the various books used; where an alternative name presented itself read-ability was again the final judge.

FURTHER READING

Jean Doresse, *Ethiopia* (London: Elek Books, 1959).

A. H. M. Jones and Elizabeth Monroe, *A History of Ethiopia* (Oxford: Oxford University Press, 1966).

Richard K.P.P. Pankhurst (ed.), *The Ethiopian Royal Chronicles* (Addis Ababa: Oxford University Press, 1967).

Timothy Severin, *The African Adventure* (London: Hamish Hamilton, 1973).

Edward Ullendorf, *The Ethiopians* (London: Oxford University Press, 1973).

6
Nzinga of Angola

ABOUT 1581–1663

Both within Angola and elsewhere throughout Africa there is a growing literature about Nzinga as well as a wealth of oral stories and myths. So powerful is her legend that a prehistoric imprint of a footprint on a rock in the natural fortress of Pungu Andongo[1] near the Cuanza river is known as Queen Jinga's footprint, as if her very feet could mark solid stone.

Mistaking the title of the ruler (or *ngola*) of Ndongo for the name of his country, the Portuguese called the kingdom of the Mbundu tribe Angola, the name by which it is known to this day. The first contacts between the Mbundu and the Europeans were friendly: the Ngola Kiluanji made it clear that he welcomed trade but did not want his country disrupted by the mass conversions to Christianity that the Portuguese had undertaken in the neighbouring kingdom of Kongo. In fact, in the early part of the sixteenth century Ndongo flourished largely due to the profits of the Portuguese-promoted slave trade. Kiluanji took the opportunity to dispose of criminals and prisoners of war without needing to enslave many of his people. But, as had happened in Kongo, the demands of the colony of Brazil in Latin America for more and more workers soon put pressure on the Portuguese governor of the coastal port of Luanda to find more slaves. The governor, Paulo Dias de Novais, left the slave trade in the hands of the Jesuit priests; his main concern was to find the legendary silver mines in the interior.

The early slave trade had increased the Ngola Kiluanji's wealth and enabled him to conquer some land around his borders. Disputes over these new territories, however, brought him into conflict with the Portuguese. It was one of these quarrels over the Ilamba territory, that created the rift between the former allies.

War broke out in 1581 and was to last for nearly a hundred years. (It was while these early battles were raging that Kiluanji's daughter, the Princess Nzinga, was born.) Fortunately for the Mbundu, Kiluanji was a great fighter and although the Portuguese

were able to lay waste to his border territories, even a combined
Portuguese–Kongo invasion was defeated.

Kiluanji had five children, two girls and three boys, though the
eldest was considered illegitimate. Of the five, Nzinga resembled
her father the most, but her early adult life was no different from
that of other royal women—she was married and had a son. The
upheaval came some time around 1618. Despite his success as a
warrior, Kiluanji was a tyrant and his increasingly wayward
behaviour finally angered his people and led to his overthrow. He
was deposed and killed, and Mbandi, the illegitimate eldest son,
made himself *ngola*.

The difficult years

Mbandi proceeded to silence all opposition: he killed not only his
younger brother but also Nzinga's son (she was never to have
children again). He continued, even to the point of killing the chiefs
who had supported his succession. Realizing that her half-brother
was capable of any cruelty, Nzinga left Mbamba, the Ndongo capital, with her husband and sisters and settled in the neighbouring
territory of Matamba.

Had the Ngola Mbandi been as fierce with the Portuguese as he
had been with his own family, Nzinga might have accepted the
situation, but he turned out to be a weakling. At the advance of the
Portuguese, searching for the secrets of the silver mines, Mbandi
fled, surrendering the heartland of Ndongo to the Europeans. He
retreated to an island on the river Cuanza and sent word to his
sister, asking her to help him by negotiating a treaty with the
Portuguese. His only hope, or so he believed, was to make peace.

The murder of her son would have been sufficient reason for
Nzinga to have refused her brother's request and to have done what
she could to save herself and her sisters. But her greatest desire was
to defend her people and their land from the white men and to that
end she put aside all thoughts of the family quarrel and set off with
her servants to Luanda.

A famous meeting

Nzinga's position was extremely delicate: her brother had surrendered everything (the Portuguese had even appointed a puppet
ngola) and yet she was expected to negotiate a settlement. But she
was a natural diplomat and realized that her only hope was to brave
it out. Her meeting with the new governor, João Correa de Souza,
has become a legend in the history of Africa's confrontations with

13 Queen Nzinga's famous meeting with the Portuguese Governor in Luanda, from a Dutch engraving of that time

Europe. Nzinga organized her arrival at the governor's residence in such a way that no one could be in any doubt that this was a 'royal' occasion and not the humble arrival of a conquered messenger. Musicians heralded her approach as she entered the audience chamber escorted by her serving women. Now occurred the event that was to make her so famous, an event happily recorded by a Dutch artist a little while later. There was only one chair, the governor's throne. Nzinga was determined not to be placed at a disadvantage. Summoning one of her women, who came forward and fell to her hands and knees, the haughty princess sat down on this human seat. When Governor de Souza entered, he found himself already outmanoeuvred. During the following interview he was not allowed to regain the upper hand.

Over the years of fighting, the Mbundu had taken a number of Portuguese prisoners. When de Souza asked for their return, however, Nzinga smilingly agreed, provided all the Mbundu who had been carried off to Brazil and elsewhere were brought back in exchange. It was clearly an impossible condition and after much discussion the solution was a treaty whereby Portugal would recognize the Ngola Mbandi as ruler of an independent Ndongo kingdom and would withdraw its army. In return, the Mbundu would return the Portuguese prisoners, help the Europeans with the slave trade and take part in joint efforts to resist the Jaga. (The Jaga were a group of migratory cannibals who had devastated Kongo. They were not a tribe but a roving band of escaped slaves and criminals. They elected their chiefs, captured children rather than marrying and having their own, and lived in war camps. They were now becoming an increasing problem further south.) It was a treaty on equal terms and Nzinga accepted it as such. When she finally rose from her 'chair' she must have been satisfied.

Conversion

Probably as part of a private agreement intended to reinforce the treaty, Nzinga stayed on in Luanda in order to receive instruction in the Christian faith. Such a move was more political than religious. Indeed the Jesuit priests concerned were deeply implicated in the slave trade. They officiated at daily mass baptisms in the docks, where lines of captives shuffling into the ships were first sprinkled with holy water and given a new name. But Nzinga knew that her status as a 'Christian' ally of Portugal would entitle her people to favoured treatment. Her baptism in the cathedral at Luanda would have been attended by a good deal of public ceremonial. She chose as her Christian name Dona Anna de Souza in order to strengthen her links with the governor.

She returned to Ndongo but it was soon to become apparent that her efforts were not to be rewarded. Governor de Souza may have wished to carry out his side of the bargain but the pressures from Lisbon and Brazil to increase the slave trade were too strong for any individual to resist. In any case his first contact with the *ngola* had been a disaster. He had promised to send a priest to Ndongo but when the man arrived he turned out to be an African convert. The Mbundu were not interested in the Christian religion for its own sake; they wanted contact with the Portuguese and a *white* priest was what they needed. To Nzinga it was obvious that these moves would not lead to the return of their lands. She set off to Luanda again in the hope of getting the treaty enforced.

There was now a new governor as de Souza had been recalled after a quarrel with the Jesuits. Her discussions with him convinced her that there was no way that she could come to terms with the slave-hungry Portuguese. She returned to tell her brother that they must fight for their country. Unfortunately, the Ngola Mbandi had no such intentions. It was now increasingly apparent that his sister had inherited their father's spirit. The people looked to her for the leadership he failed to provide. Trying to anticipate any move on her part to replace him, he left his base for Luanda where he knelt down before the governor and asked for Portuguese protection to re-inforce his authority over his own people.

Nzinga now determined to do away with this treacherous weakling and at the same time strike a blow against the Portuguese. Her political solution was brilliant: she formed an alliance with the Jaga, undoubtedly the most warlike people in the region. That Nzinga managed to forge a working army out of what had been a group of uncontrollable murderers is extraordinary. Her first step was to kill the wretched Mbandi on his return from Luanda. Suspecting her anger, he had sent his son away, but Nzinga now persuaded the Jaga leader, Kaza Kangola, to capture Mbandi's boy. When he handed him over to his aunt she had him poisoned.

Cannibalism

It is from this event and the subsequent deaths that the legend of Nzinga, the cannibal queen, has grown. Naturally it was a legend that her Portuguese enemies were only too happy to foster. It was said that she ate her dead brother's liver and then when she proclaimed herself *ngola*, the ceremonies turned into a cannibal orgy. The truth is that in order to resist the guns and cannon of the white slavers she was obliged to accept the Jaga as her allies and to tolerate their practices. Far from being a murderess her main aim was to end the enslavement of her people. It was her refusal to hand back escaped slaves that prompted the Portuguese finally to occupy Ndongo and make it a vassal state, setting up one of her close relatives, Ari Kiluanji, as the puppet *ngola*. Despite this her people were willing to leave their land and follow a woman leader, which shows that she was not a bloodthirsty monster.

Her tactics for resisting the outnumbered but better-armed Portuguese have been much admired and even imitated successfully in this century. She formed her people into a guerrilla army. By keeping them on the move she was able to avoid a disastrous battle while harassing her enemies wherever they least expected it. She used the island in the Cuanza as a base whenever she could, though occasionally the Portuguese would force her to move. In late 1629 and early 1630 she promised to marry the Jaga chief and with this strengthened alliance moved east to Matamba where she defeated the ruling queen and created a new land for herself and her people. Between 1630 and 1635 she built up her new country. It was free of tribalism in the sense that it was not dominated by one people, for she merged her Mbundu with any Jaga who wished to settle, along with slaves escaping from the Portuguese.

Nzinga began sending out war parties from Matamba to attack the settlements of the Ngola Ari, the traitor. But her situation was not easy; she was forced to break with the Jaga chief when he plundered the Mbundu capital of Matamba. Despite the fragility of the alliance there was one hopeful sign. Divisions also existed among the Europeans, and the Portuguese were now under pressure from the Dutch who were keen to increase their share of the African trade.

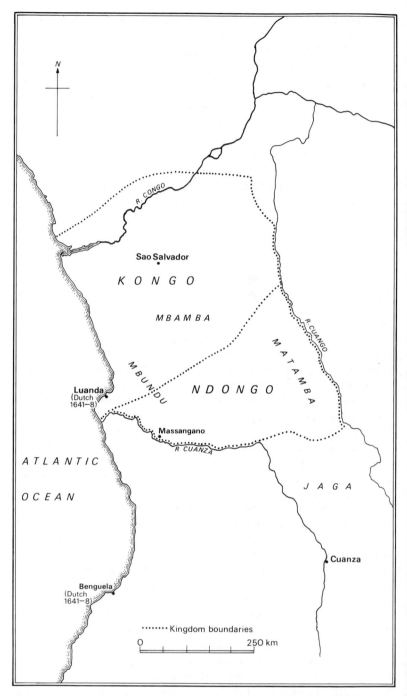

The Kingdoms of Kongo and Ndongo in the sixteenth century

The Dutch

Aware that Dutch vessels were trading along the coast and not wishing to have an enemy inland, the Portuguese now remembered their treaty with Nzinga. They had, they now admitted, been unjust; they must recreate the alliance. In 1639 it was Nzinga's turn to receive embassies from the Portuguese. In the end nothing came of them. The Portuguese were incapable of carrying out their promises and Nzinga continued to attack their towns whenever she could.

Seeing the success of her resistance and encouraged by the Dutch advance, the *manikongo*, Garcia II of Kongo, decided that his people should also fight. The Portuguese now found themselves with three enemies. In 1641 an army was raised to suppress Kongo while plans were made to invade Matamba. But they were too late. In August the Dutch arrived at Luanda. The Portuguese retreated to the interior.

It was only a matter of time before reinforcements from Brazil would enable the Portuguese to retake Luanda, but for four years Nzinga did everything possible to break down their resistance. The Dutch built forts on the coast which kept the Portuguese landlocked for the moment. But the Portuguese still had their guns and cannon and any direct attack by Nzinga would have been defeated.

In 1645 Nzinga decided that a risk was necessary and she surrounded the Portuguese forces in the settlement at Massangano. But she had not taken into account the desperation of the defenders, many of whom were criminals and murderers exiled from Portugal. Not only did they manage to break out in the January of the following year but they went on to attack Nzinga's camp, killing 2,000 of her people and capturing her sisters, Barbara and Engracia. The Portuguese governor then sent a relief army which resulted in a further defeat for Nzinga.

She was soon fighting back again. With the aid of Dutch and Kongo reinforcements she won several small battles. She might have gone on to victory if the Jaga had not chosen that moment to break the alliance. Angry at the loss of income caused by the disruption of the slave trade, they went over to the enemy. Nzinga, however, still managed to harass the remaining Portuguese and they were almost defeated when in 1648 the long-awaited reinforcements set sail from Rio de Janeiro. Now the allies were on the defensive, but Nzinga fought alongside the Dutch until their defeat when the Portuguese retook Luanda.

We know something of the details of Nzinga's life at this time from the dispatches of Captain Füller, the Dutch military attaché who accompanied her. He described how everyone fell to their knees and kissed the ground at her approach, a strange sight for women did not usually hold power. She was obliged to dress as a man and kept a 'harem' of young men dressed as women who were her 'wives'. Although she was advised by a council of elders, Füller makes it clear that she was the military strategist and although past sixty led her warriors herself.

Survival

After the Dutch defeat the *manikongo* broke the alliance and did homage to the Portuguese. There was nothing for Nzinga to do but retreat to the highlands of Matamba. She continued the struggle as before by guerrilla actions, retreating into the hills whenever the enemy retaliated. These were hard years; her sister Dona Engracia had been strangled by the Portuguese while Dona Barbara remained a prisoner. But she fought on. The result of her resistance was a new country. Although she never recovered Ndongo, Matamba became a settled land where even the treacherous Jaga gave up their cannibalism and merged with the Mbundu to form one nation. Prepared to use any means to ensure the survival of the infant state the aged queen decided to accept Portuguese overtures for some sort of peace. She accepted rebaptism, a small price to pay, and in exchange for 130 slaves her sister was released after nearly eleven years in captivity. At the age of seventy-five Nzinga decided to 'settle down' at last! She disbanded her 'harem' and formally married one of the youngest 'wives'. Almost unique among women rulers she decided that she would be succeeded by another woman, her sister, and to reinforce this plan Dona Barbara was married to Don Antonio, the general of the armies.

Secure at last, Nzinga established increasing contact with the Portuguese. She sent an embassy to the Pope in Rome and when his reply came, she ordered a festival to honour the occasion. Although by now over eighty, Nzinga took a part in the entertainment. Perhaps more secure of her position, she dressed as a woman though as an Amazon (a female warrior) in a mock battle between her groups of ladies.

She died on 17 December 1663 aged about eighty-two. The nation that she had created survived her and Dona Barbara and her descendants ruled over the land of Matamba. None, however, could remove the lurking Portuguese menace. The nineteenth century saw the establishment of European power all over Africa and the last vestiges of independence were removed from Angola. A complete colonial system was imposed. The resistance to that system in this century bore a remarkable resemblance to Nzinga's methods. The long guerrilla campaign that led to Angolan independence may have had more and better weapons but in essentials it was not so different from its predecessor three hundred years before. Nor was the connection unremarked, for the story of the queen who never surrendered has long been a source of inspiration to her successors.

NOTES
[1] J. and I. Rudner, *The Hunter and His Art* (Cape Town: C. Struick, 1970).

FURTHER READING
Florence T. Polatnik and Albert L. Saleton, *Shapers of Africa* (New York: Julian Messner, 1969).
David Sweetman, *Queen Nzinga* (London: Longman, 1971).
Douglas L. Wheeler and René Pelissier, *Angola* (London: Pall Mall Press, 1971).

7
Dona Beatrice of Kongo

ABOUT 1682–1706

In 1706 in São Salvador, the capital of the kingdom of Kongo in what is today Angola, a young woman was led out into a public square and burned to death, her baby in her arms. This cruel execution was the only way the authorities in Kongo could deal with a woman who had threatened their very existence. She was known to the people as Dona Beatrice and the reason that the king and his foreign advisers feared her was that ordinary people believed that God had spoken to her—His message was that Kongo should be reborn, free of the Europeans whose slave trade had reduced it to misery.

Three hundred years earlier, the kingdom of Kongo lying on either side of the lower river Zaïre and covering most of modern northern Angola had been the most powerful of the states on the west coast of central Africa.

One fact that has always intrigued historians is that, unlike most other parts of Africa, the early contacts with Europe, far from destroying the kingdom of Kongo, were peaceful and advantageous to both sides. The first meetings with the Portuguese in 1482 seemed to herald an era of friendship and progress. No sooner had the Portuguese arrived at the capital, Mbanza Kongo, in 1491 than the *manikongo* (or king) at the time insisted on being baptized a Christian and even took the name of the Portuguese king, John. But it was John's second son, Affonso, who was to attempt the total transformation of Kongo into a Christian kingdom when he became *manikongo* sometime around 1507.

To the Portuguese, Affonso was a near perfect creature who lived to further the cause of Christ, building churches, renaming his capital São Salvador and generally doing all in his power to 'Europeanize' his people. So keen was he to train all his subjects in the new ways that he opened a school for girls run by one of his sisters. The story of how the relationship between the king and the Portuguese deteriorated is often depicted as a tragedy that need never have happened if only the Portuguese had tried harder and their greed for slaves had been less overwhelming. But the misconceptions were not one-sided for Affonso seems to have identified Christianity with power in a way that would have surprised the Portuguese priests had they realized it.

As in Angola the Portuguese wanted slaves for their South American colony of Brazil. There were no slaves in Kongo or its neighbours, though there had been a form of serfdom, usually temporary, as a punishment for crime or as a way of paying off debts. Affonso agreed to sell serfs to the Portuguese, but very quickly the missionaries became slave dealers. Wishing to please them Affonso made war on his neighbours to capture prisoners to be sold as slaves. Most of these wars were directed against Kongo's southern neighbour, the kingdom of Ndongo, and continued after Affonso's death. In 1556 the army of Affonso's son, the Manikongo Diogo, was defeated. Diogo died fighting against another of his neighbours and his successor ruled over a kingdom so weak that the Jaga, the group of wandering cannibals who also invaded Ndongo, were able to overrun it at one point. Slavery had reduced Kongo to a ruin at the centre of which Affonso's successors presided over the travesty of a mock-European court.

14   The King of Kongo receiving European ambassadors, from a
     seventeenth-century Dutch engraving

By the end of the seventeenth century internal rivalries had reduced Kongo to poverty and despair. A Capuchin priest, Laurent de Lucques, wrote in 1701:

> The news coming from the Kongo is always worse and the enmities between the royal houses are tearing the kingdom further and further apart. At present there are four kings of the Kongo. There are also two great dukes of Mamba; three great dukes in Ovando; two great dukes in Batta and four marquises of Enchus. The authority of each is declining and they are destroying each other by making war among themselves. Each claims to be chief. They make raids on one another in order to steal and to sell their prisoners like animals.[1]

São Salvador was falling into ruin and most of its population had fled. Yet in the midst of these disasters an unexpected revival took place.

Visions and prophecies

It was not surprising that many people resented the way their country had declined into lawlessness and wished to see a return to the days of Affonso. Many people came to believe that a religious revival would restore the country to the happy days when the first Portuguese had helped create the Christian kingdom before the slave trade. The result was an upsurge of religious fanaticism in which prophets and prophetesses revealed visions that mixed religion and politics in ways that fitted in with the people's dreams. A woman claimed to have received a message from the Virgin Mary in which the Mother of Christ spoke of her anger at what had happened in Kongo. A young man proclaimed that God would punish the people unless São Salvador was rebuilt. Strangest of all, an old woman, Ma-Futa, claimed to possess the head of Christ disfigured by man's wickedness—it was in fact a stone from the Ambriz river.

In a vision of the Virgin Mary, Ma-Futa learned of the disasters predicted unless the *manikongo* reoccupied the capital. The queen believed that Ma-Futa had miraculous healing powers and the rumour that she was a saint began to spread. When the missionaries tried to bring her to 'justice' the *manikongo* asserted himself and protected her.

But these events were only a foretaste of the true religious revival that was to galvanize Kongo. There now appeared a woman who was to attempt a national revival by means of her own version of the Christian faith.

Dona Beatrice

Kimpa Vita, as she was first called, was of noble birth, a Mukongo aristocrat, a 'priestess' of the cult of Marinda, used to the ways of power and the intrigues of the ruling élite. She must have been well aware of the failure of that élite and to have acutely observed the way someone like Ma-Futa could sway minds and order events. That was precisely what she, as Dona Beatrice, determined to do.

As she later described it, it began when she was sick, dying, and St Anthony appeared to her. There was nothing accidental about this choice of saint—St Anthony was a Portuguese saint and especially revered by missionaries and settlers in Kongo and Ndongo. But this was no 'white' apparition for St Anthony appeared to Dona Beatrice in the form of one of her brothers. In one person, the foreign religion was given an African personality. This was what Dona Beatrice wanted. Her aim was the restoration of the kingdom as it was romantically believed to have been in its glory under Affonso I.

Like many mystics she renounced material things. She even imitated the death of Christ—her followers came to believe that she died on Friday, went to heaven to plead the cause of her people with God and was resurrected on Sunday. Her political message, that Kongo must be reborn, and the appeal of the religious imagery that surrounded it, was instantly adopted by most who heard her preach.

She believed passionately that São Salvador should again know the glorious days when it had been 'the city of the bells'. By 1704 she was established in the capital, recognized as both a religious and political leader. A Capuchin priest, a Father Bernardo de Gallo, drew her portrait, wearing a gold crown and green garments, and his colleague Laurent de Lucques described her:

> This young woman was about twenty-two years old. She was rather slender and fine-featured. Externally she appeared very devout. She spoke with gravity and seemed to weigh each word. She foretold the future and predicted, among other things, that the day of Judgement was near.[2]

She was so honoured in São Salvador that the lords offered the ends of their capes as tablecloths for her to eat off. Wherever she went a retinue of noble women cleared a path before her.

Her achievement was to create an African church with the traditional Bible stories as background: Kongo was the Holy Land; Christ had been born in São Salvador; the founders of Christianity were Africans. Most important, rather than copying the whites, as the manikongo and his nobles had done, Dona Beatrice insisted on the

15   Statuette of St Anthony dating from the early years of Christianity in the Kingdom of Kongo

basic difference of black people. The whites were originally made from a certain soft stone, while the blacks came from a sort of fig-tree. In less than two years this young prophetess had created a new church with its own dogma. The central part of her beliefs would be described today as *négritude* or *black consciousness*, an awareness of the value of the African experience. There was a return to wearing the traditional bark-cloth garments instead of adaptations of European dress. The Christian message had originally been adopted in Kongo to give the power of Europe to the *manikongo*— which it manifestly had not done. Now Dona Beatrice took that message and reworked it to give power to the people. She proclaimed the imminent arrival of a golden age for the true believer when São Salvador would be rebuilt, repopulated and filled with all that anyone might desire.

Her most telling alteration of Christianity was to permit polygamy, opposition to which had so isolated the Portuguese missionaries from the heart of Bukongo culture. But she was no libertarian and other rules were strict and aimed at disciplining the people for the greater strength of the country. The European missionaries named her faith Antonianism, after her saintly vision. Needless to say they were utterly opposed to it.

At first there was little they could do for, as Bernardo de Gallo recorded, she was extraordinarily successful:

Thus it came about that São Salvador was rapidly populated, for some went there to worship the pretended saint, others to see the rebuilt capital, some to see friends, others attracted by the desire to recover their health miraculously, others still out of political ambition and to be the first to occupy the place. In this manner the false saint became the restorer, ruler, and lord of the Congo.[3]

In the eyes of her followers, she had acquired such divine power that as she passed fallen trees would straighten. Yet despite all this she was brought down. The Portuguese were determined to destroy her and when it came her fall was rapid.

The authority of Manikongo Pedro IV had so declined that a rival group of nobles had set up their own *manikongo* in opposition. Pedro IV needed Portuguese support to maintain his weakened position and he was under great pressure from the missionaries to silence Dona Beatrice and suppress the Antonine movement. The Capuchin missionaries were able to persuade Pedro that Dona Beatrice was a supporter of his rival, but he was able to move against her only when she herself had undermined her own position. Wishing to re-enact a full Africanization of the Christian story she gave birth to a son, claiming that she remained a virgin. Despite the awe in which she was held, this story seems to have weakened her hold on her people's faith. Just after the birth, in the early months of 1706, Pedro had her arrested, though not without some fear as to what the popular reaction might be. His first idea was to send her to the bishop of Angola for trial, probably hoping that she would escape on her way to Luanda. But the Capuchins wanted her dealt with publicly and they forced Pedro to have her tried by the royal council. She was sentenced to be burned at the stake.

Laurent de Lucques described her death:

Two men with bells in their hands went and stood in the middle of this great multitude and gave a signal with their bells, and immediately the people fell back and in the middle of the empty space the basciamucano, that is, the judge, appeared. He was clad from head to foot in a black mantle and on his head he wore a hat which was also black, a black so ugly that I do not believe its like for ugliness has ever been seen. The culprits were led before him. The young woman, who carried her child in her arms now appeared to be filled with fear and dread. The accused ones sat on the bare ground and awaited their death sentence.

We understood then that they had decided to burn the child along with his mother. This seemed to us too great a cruelty. I hastened to speak to the king to see whether there was some way to save him . . . .

The basciamucano made a long speech. Its principal theme was a eulogy of the king. He enumerated his titles and gave proofs of his zeal for justice. Finally he pronounced the sentence against Dona Beatriz, saying that under the false name of Saint Anthony she had deceived the people with her heresies and falsehoods. Consequently the king, her lord, and the royal council condemned her to die at the stake. The woman did all she could to recant, but her efforts were in vain. There arose such a great tumult among the multitude that it was impossible for us to be of assistance to the two condemned persons. They were quickly led to the stake. For the rest, all we can say is that there was gathered there a great pile of wood on which they were thrown. They were covered with other pieces of wood and burned alive. Not content with this, the following morning some men came again and burned the bones that remained and reduced everything to very fine ashes.[4]

It was a hollow victory. Far from ending the 'heresy' Dona Beatrice's death was the beginning of a new stage in the spread of Antonianism. The faithful believed that where Dona Beatrice and her son had died two deep wells appeared, each containing a beautiful star. The relics found among the ashes of the 'saint' became revered objects. In a way she could not have foreseen, Dona Beatrice's aim of strengthening her country under the leadership of a powerful ruler was to be achieved. Two years after her death Pedro IV was forced to organize an army to suppress the Antonianists. Ironically, this gave him new strength and after his victory the country was temporarily united.

There is, however, little evidence that Dona Beatrice's influence as a liberator continued in the way that Queen Nzinga's did. Ultimately Kongo continued its decline until it was finally absorbed into the Portuguese colony of Angola in the nineteenth century. Dona Beatrice is of great interest to us today as the first of several early pioneers of Africanism, pioneers who saw clearly the need to restore to the people of the African continent a belief in themselves.

NOTES
[1] Jean Cuvelier, *Relations sur le Congo du père Laurent de Lucques (1700–17)* (Brussels: 1953), p. 146.
[2] Ibid.,pp. 231–2.
[3] Louis Jadin, *Le Congo et la secte des Antoniens* (Brussels: 1961), pp. 96–7.
[4] Cuvelier, op. cit., pp. 235–8.

FURTHER READING
Georges Balandier, *The Kingdom of the Kongo* (London: George Allen and Unwin, 1968).
Peter Forbath, *The River Congo* (London: Secker and Warburg, 1978).

8
Mmanthatisi of the Sotho

ABOUT 1781–1835

Sometime in the years between 1780 and 1782 a daughter was born to one of the wives of Mothaba, the chief of the Sia, one of the two main branches of the Sotho-speaking peoples who lived in what is now the Orange Free State in the Republic of South Africa. The girl, Monyale, was married to Mokotjo, chief of the senior Sotho group, the Tlokwa. The event had probably been planned early in her life as the two groups were closely knit. Monyale's new mother-in-law, Mmamane, was also her aunt. As the daughter of a chief, Monyale became Mokotjo's 'great wife', senior to the other two wives, and she bore him two future chiefs, Sekonyela and Mota. It was after the birth of their daughter, Ntatise, that in accordance with custom Monyale's name was changed to Mmanthatisi, the name by which she is known to history.

Mmanthatisi is unusual in that she led her people herself during one of the greatest crises in southern African history. Her husband, Mokotjo, had died in 1817, probably of illness, and she found herself faced with a succession struggle. Her eldest son, Sekonyela, was only about thirteen years old; he had not yet been circumcized and was not immediately eligible for the chieftainship. Her brother-in-law, Sehalahala, seemed set to inherit, but Mmanthatisi was determined to prevent this and persuaded the elders of the group to accept her as regent. Women rulers were rare among the Sotho but not unknown; her mother-in-law Mmamane had ruled in Mokotjo's name for a time and certain sections of the Sotho had women regiments led by chiefs' daughters, though whether the young Monyale had been such a warrior we do not know.

Her appointment as regent for her son did not put an end to opposition. The following years were a constant struggle against her brother-in-law and his supporters. When the time for Sekonyela's circumcision arrived she realized that he was now in danger. She therefore sent him to her own people, the Sia, where the ceremonies could be performed in safety. There were numerous border conflicts at this time and they gave her the experience that she needed to cope with the upheaval whose first tremors were beginning to be felt.

The Mfecane

The crisis that was to engulf southern Africa was caused by the pressures of land shortage and propelled by the rise of Zulu power under Shaka. Until the middle of the eighteenth century there had been land enough in Africa for the roaming Bantu groups who slowly pressed southwards whenever new grazing lands were needed for their herds of cattle. But the march north from the Cape of the European Boers in search of farming land finally cut off this age-old migration. War between the different groupings became inevitable. However, the sheer ferocity of one of these groups, the Zulu, whom Shaka had trained into a deadly, invincible fighting force, created a whirlwind reaction that no one could have anticipated. It began among the Nguni peoples of which the Zulu were a part. Reacting to Shaka's wars of conquest, which were to carve out one of Africa's largest empires, the defeated Nguni groups spread into the lands of other groups, setting up a chain reaction called the *mfecane*—the crushing. Whole peoples moved as far north as modern Tanzania. The results were horrendous as can be seen from this description by Donald R. Morris:

> As each clan was shaken loose, it attacked a fresh area, and the groups of refugees grew smaller and smaller, and their courses shorter, until something over two and a half-million people were stumbling back and forth over the land, sometimes running away from something, and sometimes striving to reach something, but always in search of food and a security that no longer existed. Over scores of thousands of square miles, not a single permanent Kraal existed, not a single clan staunch enough to avoid being sucked into the maelstrom. Cannibalism, which was fully as repugnant to Bantu civilization as it is to our own, became common, and reached the point where entire clans depended on it and nothing else to feed themselves. Nameless, formless mobs coalesced and began to move, acquiring strength from individuals who saw the only hope of safety in numbers, and these mobs rolled across the blighted country and stripped it of everything edible. For decades their aimless tracks were marked by countless human bones.[1]

This became a time of individual leaders as never before in Bantu history. Chiefs had often been mere figureheads with little power and could even be displaced if they dissatisfied their people. Now strong rulers were needed. It was through them that the Bantu states were carved out, often led by tyrants able to dominate the wretched displaced masses they controlled, but occasionally led by an exceptional leader of vigour and compassion such as Moshweshwe, the founder-king of Lesotho. The Tlokwa were lucky; they had Mmanthatisi to lead them at the very moment when this storm was gathering force.

Chain reaction

Shaka's army had defeated a group led by Zwide who was thus forced from his lands. Zwide in turn attacked Mmanthatisi's people but her husband was able to defend them in a battle just before his death in 1817. Zwide took what remained of his army and attacked and defeated another Nguni group led by Matiwane. Matiwane's group moved into the lands of their neighbours who in turn set off north under their leader, Mpangazita, towards Mmanthatisi's territory. Mpangazita did not expect a woman to resist in the way that Mmanthatisi did when the collision occurred in about 1822.

The two sides were equally matched and after an initial bloody encounter both broke away in different directions. But Mpangazita managed to get away with most of the Tlokwa food and cattle. Mmanthatisi was forced to lead her uprooted people without supplies to her original homeland among the Sia.

The great horde

So vast a horde could not stay without ruining their hosts and so began that long and bitter search for a new home that all the victims of the *mfecane* suffered. The great multitude of men, women and children made its way westward, south of the Vaal river, attacking all who lay before them. After about a year Sekonyela, now aged about nineteen, was able to lead a regiment. There is no doubt, however, that Mmanthatisi was the overall commander, although she was unlikely to have led military expeditions herself. So successful and so feared was she that her warriors were called Mantatees after her, a name that spread far beyond the lands they devastated. After only two years she and her Tlokwa followers had scattered three of the other vast, roaming groups that they encountered on their travels. We know from the records of Europeans outside the region that it seemed as if the entire misery of the *mfecane* was her doing, so successful was she in holding her people together. Stationed at a mission on the edge of the Kgalagadi desert, the Reverend Robert Moffat wrote:

For more than a year, numerous and strange reports have at intervals reached us, some indeed of such a character as induced us to treat them as the reveries of a madman. It was said that a mighty woman, of the name of Mantatee, was at the head of an invisible army, numerous as locusts, marching onward among the interior nations, carrying devastation and ruin wherever she went; that she nourished the army with her own milk, sent out hornets before it, and in one word, was laying the world desolate.[3]

Other sources added the detail that she had a single great eye set in the middle of her forehead. We now know that these writers were crediting her with the activities of others, for there were two other leaders as successful as she was in holding their peoples together. These were Mpangazita and Matiwane, the latter again on the move having been forced out of Mpangazita's territory by Shaka's continuing expansion. She was also blamed for the damage caused by groups led by Moletsane and Sebitwane.

Into Lesotho

Destroying peoples as it went, Mmanthatisi's increasing multitude entered the Caledon valley in present-day Lesotho. As they moved only the soldiers could be fed from the central supplies. The rest—women, children, the aged—were obliged to scavenge as best they could; many were abandoned to die as the great sea of people swept onwards. It was this that probably saved the young Moshweshwe when the Tlokwa entered his lands. So keen were they on looting the farms that lay before them that he was able to defeat and drive them back in what was called the Battle of the Pots—Mmanthatisi's people having had all their cooking pots destroyed during the battle.

The Tlokwa moved on but there was no forethought as to where they were headed. The only thing that a leader like Mmanthatisi could hope to do was to hold her people together and survive the attacks of other, similar, hordes. She was unaware that the great curving movement that her people were making was about to bring her up against Mpangazita again. The two enormous groups clashed not far from Maseru, the capital of today's Lesotho. Despite some brilliant fighting by her warriors the battle was not a success for the Tlokwa—Mmanthatisi was obliged to lead her people to safety across the Caledon river where they spent the night. When dawn broke she saw that her enemies had gone. Her people were now desperately hungry and she despatched every available warrior to forage for food. No sooner had they gone than Mpangazita sprang his trap—he had moved his men under cover of darkness to the hills behind her, and they were now pouring down

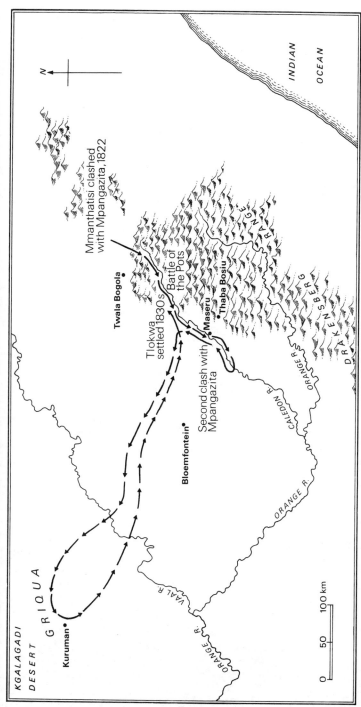

Sketch map to show the extent of Mmanthatisi's wanderings during the *mfecane*

the slopes. This was to be Mmanthatisi's greatest moment. Without hesitation she rounded up every woman and child in the great camp, along with every single head of cattle that could be caught, and stretched them out in a long, thin line. Then, with as much noise as possible, she drove people and cattle at the enemy. To Mpangazita's warriors what now appeared through the dust was an endless line of Tlokwa coming at them prepared for battle. They turned and fled; Mmanthatisi had saved her people from almost certain massacre.

Final settlement

The great Tlokwa horde rolled on but by now resistance to them was beginning. When they reached what was then Bechuanaland, Makaba of the Ngwaketsi was able to drive them off. When they reached the fringes of the Kgalagadi the missionary, Robert Moffat, was able to persuade the Griqua, a race of half-caste Khoikhoi, to use their guns to protect the local people. Mmanthatisi now crossed the Vaal river and led her people across the blighted plains of the Orange Free State. Weakened by hunger and the ravages of wandering groups of bandits the Tlokwa were no longer a match for Matiwane's horde, who again attacked them. Fleeing as best they could, they made their way back to the Caledon valley in Lesotho.

Mmanthatisi now decided to give up the struggle and to make a new home for those of her people who wished to settle down. Two neighbouring mountains, Joalaboholo and Kooaneng, on the northern side of the Caledon river were chosen. The principal settlement was on the flat top of Kooaneng, the only entrance guarded by a stone wall and narrow gate, with a plentiful supply of stones to rain down on any attackers. Some groups broke away and continued the wandering of the *mfecane*. But to those who stayed she added any remnants of the Sotho or other groups who wished to join her.

16   Stronghold of the Mantatees during the 1830s

In so doing she resembled Moshweshwe under whose technical sovereignty she and her people now were. Out of the flotsam of the *mfecane* Moshweshwe was founding the nation that was to survive him, using the mountain of Thaba Bosiu, a natural fortress, as his base.

Sekonyela was now ready to claim his inheritance. He had been named chief in about 1824 and some time in the 1830s his mother handed over full authority to him. Unfortunately he was an arrogant man who failed to realize the scope of what Moshweshwe was trying to achieve. For thirty years the two struggled for control of the Caledon valley. Moshweshwe was able to attract more followers and in 1853 he overwhelmed the Tlokwa. Sekonyela was forced to flee to Bloemfontein, then on to Cape Colony in the white-controlled south. The Tlokwa were now absorbed into Moshweshwe's new nation, a fitting end to their long struggle for survival.

The last years

After Sekonyela became chief, Mmanthatisi retired, probably to Twala Bogola near today's town of Bethlehem in South Africa. She could now assume the position that she would have held had the *mfecane* not intervened—the role of queen mother, the respected senior figure and adviser to her son. Was she in decline or did she enjoy herself after the trials of the previous years? One report, again from second-hand sources, says that she could only be seen in the morning: 'After that, native beer claimed her for its own.'[4]

As the widow of a chief she could not remarry but was allowed sexual relations with her dead husband's brothers, bearing a daughter by one of them. Her people had sometimes called her Mosayane, which means 'the little woman', but reports suggest that she was in fact bigger than the name would indicate, though not unattractive. A visiting French missionary described her sweet and agreeable expression and elegant figure, dressed in a plaited apron, covered with an ox-hide cloak and wearing a copper necklace and bangles, though there is an opposite tradition that after her retirement she was sickly and did not live long. There is no reference to her in any record after 1835, but when exactly she died we do not know. Whenever it was, she was subsequently buried at Joalaboholo, the other mountain opposite the settlement on Kooaneng. It is now a place sacred to the descendants of the Tlokwa whose chiefs gather there once a year to commemorate the past. Their very existence today is the result of the efforts of the extraordinary woman buried there. She and Moshweshwe are the two figures to emerge from the dreadful history of the *mfecane* as having achieved something for their people. Curiously, her other son, Mota, had led

17   Sekonyela, son of Mmanthatisi

another Tlokwa group eastward into Natal. After the Anglo–Zulu War of 1879 his son, Hlubi, was placed in charge of part of Zululand where various Sotho groups were able to settle. Ironically this was originally the land of Matiwane whose move against Mpangazita and the subsequent invasion of Sotho territory had first driven Mmanthatisi and her people from their home.

NOTES
[1] Donald R. Morris, *The Washing of the Spears* (London: Cape, 1966), pp. 56, 57.
[2] A. T. Bryant, *Olden Times in Zululand and Natal* (London: Longman, 1929).
[3] Robert Moffat, *Missionary Labours and Scenes in Southern Africa* (London, 1842), p. 340, quoted in *The Oxford History of South Africa*, p. 396.
[4] Graham Mackeurtan, *The Cradle Days of Natal* (London: Longman, 1931), pp. 232, 233.

FURTHER READING
Peter Becker, *Path of Blood* (London: Longman, 1962).
Monica Wilson and Leonard Thompson, *The Oxford History of South Africa*, vol. 1 (London: Oxford University Press, 1969).

9
Ranavalona I of Madagascar

RULED 1828–61

Ranavalona was the wife of King Radama I of Madagascar, the vast island off the east coast of Africa whose inhabitants are a mixture of Bantu peoples and waves of immigrants from south-east Asia. During the thirty tumultuous years of her reign she was able to stem the tide of European power and keep foreigners at bay. At her death on 16 August 1861 they began the penetration of her nation. It was almost a century before her people could regain their independence.

Radama was the king of the Merina peoples of the central plateau and he, as his father before him, had tried to conquer the whole island. He was supported by the British who, from their colony of Mauritius to the east, wished to keep the French out of Madagascar. Under the prompting of successive British advisers the London Missionary Society was allowed to send preachers and craftsmen to train the inhabitants of the island. The Merina dialect was turned into a written language and dictionaries and Bibles were printed; local industries and manufactures were introduced and schools opened. It was like a whirlwind: too much too soon. The result was a backlash, a grouping of traditionalist forces: opposed on the one hand to the Christian religion which seemed an offence to the traditional *sampy*, the royal talismans worshipped by the Merina; and on the other to the new economic forces, including the abolition of slavery, which seriously affected a section of the *andriana*, the nobles, and some members of the *hova*, the 'middle class'.

Had Radama I lived he might have ridden out these changes and led his country into the modern age.

Queen Ranavalona I

Following a bout of fever in 1827, Radama I was ill for seven months. As his health declined, plans were made to choose a successor. His first wife, Ramavo, had decided long before his death that she was not going to be put on one side when the moment came. Radama I had no sons and Ramavo began to hint that she was sympathetic to the conservative forces among the nobles and freemen who opposed the introduction of foreign ideas. She also let it be known that Radama's father had named her as his second successor after Radama I, a rumour that helped her position.

Radama I ended his own life in a fit of depression in 1828, leaving no clear successor. He seems, however, to have wanted his daughter to marry one of his nephews and thus ensure a joint line of inheritance. To the courtiers, the nephew, who had been educated by the missionaries, seemed likely to introduce foreign ideas that would weaken their traditional powers. Ramavo received an increasing number of visitors eager to join what was becoming a definite party within the court.

On the Sunday morning when they found Radama dead, Ramavo and her supporters moved quickly. They decided to keep the death a secret for the time being. At a great *kabary* (public meeting) two days later the people were asked to swear allegiance to an unnamed successor. On 1 August 1828 a meeting of national leaders was held in the palace and it was announced that the *sampy*, the royal talismans or good-luck symbols, had chosen Ramavo. Anyone who objected was killed. Ramavo now chose the name by which history knows her, Ranavalona, which means 'the lady who has been folded'. (This is a reference to the precious silk *lambas* or scarves that are part of the Malagasy national dress, items to be guarded and worn only at ceremonial functions.)

When Ranavalona came to power she was about forty years old, short, plump and dark, though her girlhood name implies that she was light-skinned. Her first act was to put to death all possible claimants to the inheritance—the daughter, the nephew and others —and she had herself declared king for all official purposes. However, it was obvious that her advisers were to share her power. By being brought to the throne through the support of a particular faction, Ranavalona had broken the absolute power of the monarchy. She was dependent on the support of, and so had to share authority with, the leading *hova*, the wealthy but not noble families. Ironically, although these *hova* families were reactionary and opposed to outside elements, they had acquired their wealth from the new trade brought by the foreigners, though some had lost much of it when the British insisted on the abolition of Malagasy participation in the slave trade.

Radama I was given a magnificent funeral in ceremonies lasting two days before the new authorities began exercising their power. It was felt that the queen should have a guardian and so the post of official lover was created. One of the first holders of the office, Andriamihaja, probably fathered the queen's only son, who was declared to be the result of a visit in spirit form of the late king and was thus named Rakotond Radama (Radama's boy). We must not however assume that the queen was a mere figurehead; the views of her traditionalist supporters coincided with her own and her wishes were respected.

The missionaries found the royal support for their teaching and manufacturing activities that they had had since 1810 when Radama came to the throne was now withdrawn. Britain and France were informed that all treaties were ended. In August 1829 the French sent troops to Tamatave on the east coast. But they were over-confident and when they attacked a strongly defended Merina fort at nearby Foulpointe they were driven back. The Malagasy said that they had two stout protectors, 'General Hazo' and 'General Tazo', General Forest and General Fever, the two warriors that lie in wait between the coast and the high plateau. The French stayed on the coast until a revolution in France in 1830 led to the recall of the soldiers. But this victory put Malagasy in an isolated position.

The queen's government kept changing its policy on what to do about the missionaries. The traditionalists wanted them to leave but their business interests needed the skills of the missionary crafts-men. In consequence, the queen allowed her subjects to be baptized as a concession, and persuaded the missionaries to produce useful goods such as soap to reduce the level of imports. They were also persuaded to build reservoirs and roads.

However, so many came forward to be baptized and to take communion that the leading *hova* families panicked and the per-mission was withdrawn. Despite this setback the missionaries were allowed to remain until 1835 when Ranavalona called them to a meeting and told them of her intention to maintain the traditions of her ancestors. All religious teaching was forbidden. At a great *kabary* on 1 March the abolition of the Christian faith was proclaimed to the people of the capital. Those who had been baptized were ordered to confess, and known Christians were fined or removed from posi-tions of authority.

Ranavalona was happy for the missionaries to continue with their crafts and industries, but they saw no reason to stay if they could not preach the Gospel and many therefore began to leave the island. However, the ruling group realized that Merina control over the island was based on foreign recognition: indeed, some of the iso-lated Merina garrisons on the coast were supplied by foreign ships when the overland routes were dangerous. In 1836 Ranavalona sent an embassy to King William IV of England and King Louis-Philippe of France in an attempt to repair some of the damage done by her policy of shutting out foreigners. But as the members of the embassy had no authority to negotiate any sort of treaty, their journey was pointless. In any case an event occurred in 1837 that was to mark the beginning of Madagascar's total break with the missionaries and so end the association with the European powers that Radama I had built up. A Christian woman, Rasalama, refusing to deny her faith, was taken, singing hymns all the way, to Ambohipotsy, the traditional place of execution. There she was speared to death and became the first Malagasy Christian martyr. She was soon to be joined by hundreds of her fellow-believers.

Ranavalona now brought back the old methods of summary execution and trial by *tangena*, in which the accused was forced to swallow pieces of chicken containing poison from the *tangena* plant. The accused had to vomit this up to prove his or her innocence, a trial that left many who survived weakened for life. Thousands were killed or taken for the renewed slave trade on the slightest pretext, with the result that many fled to the island's semi-desert regions and turned to banditry to survive. Away from Antananarivo[1], the capital of the Merina state, the other island states were often harshly governed. Those coastal regions that rebelled were cruelly suppressed, earning the Merina the lasting hatred of the people they had conquered. Because Ranavalona had permitted a return to slavery, a trade operated by the ruling élite, there was a further reason for military action against the coastal peoples.

The ruling families were also given monopolies for the export of cattle and agricultural produce, both essential to the islands of Mauritius and Réunion. To break this monopoly traders from these two islands sent boats to remote parts of the Malagasy coast to deal directly with the local chiefs. They encouraged these non-Merina people to oppose the central government in Antananarivo, sometimes providing them with arms. Despite the fact that Ranavalona had theoretically completed the Merina conquest of Madagascar, many of her outer provinces were still not under her full control.

We must, however, remember that some of our knowledge of Ranavalona I comes from missionary sources who were unsympathetic to her genuine desire to preserve her people's culture. To them the *sampy* or royal talismans were heathen and the intricate system of social and family relations simply taboos.

The reasons why Ranavalona and her closest supporters resisted change may have been various, but they had at least one positive result: they prevented the headlong rush to abandon the past which has resulted in the unhappiness of some colonized peoples. That today's Malagasy have a strong individual culture may be due to the period of reaction and isolation under Ranavalona. However, her enemies branded her Ranavalona the Cruel and it is this reputation that has spread to the outside world.

To the puritan nineteenth-century European mind free sexual behaviour was sinful. Yet given prevailing standards, Ranavalona was hardly the monster she had been painted. The situation that she was presented with on assuming the crown was that she would have a guardian, an official consort. Her supporters, however, understood that as a woman rather than a queen her affections might lie elsewhere. In consequence she was allowed to pick such lovers as she wished. There is no hard evidence that her appetites in this direction were exceptional. Sometimes the posts of official consort and chosen lover merged, as was the case with Andriamihaja, the probable father of her son, Prince Rakoto. But Andriamihaja was an arrogant young man and also not unsympathetic to the Christians; he was assassinated some time in 1830. He was succeeded by Rainiharo, a Hova who was not only a clever politician but handsome; again for a time the posts of lover and official consort merged. Later Rainiharo was to continue as consort and chief minister while Ranavalona found other lovers. Rainiharo's house was near the queen's palace and his family took the name Andafiavaratra, meaning 'on the north side'. The Andafiavaratra family increasingly dominated Malagasy affairs from 1830 on.

One man in particular has most interested the outside world: the Frenchman Jean Laborde, who is often pictured as the queen's romantic companion. The truth is not so dramatic. Despite Ranavalona's opposition to the activities of foreigners in her land there were certain exceptions such as the Frenchman Napoléon de Lastelle. In 1829 he was permitted to run a sugar plantation on the east coast because he shared the profits from what he produced, a sort of rum, with the queen. He also became a principal trading operator between Madagascar, Réunion and France, a venture profitable enough to the ruling élite to exempt him from the general opposition to outsiders.

Jean Laborde was an escaped convict aged twenty-five when in 1831 he arrived in Madagascar. He made his way to de Lastelle's plantation and via his fellow-countryman was introduced to the queen. Laborde was inventive and skilful. The queen for her part needed a whole range of goods that had become unavailable since the break with the foreigners. The result was a one-man industrial revolution, beginning in 1835, with Laborde setting up a manufacturing town at Mantasoa, 80 kilometres from the capital. At its height this manufacturing complex had 1,200 workmen, producing an amazing range of goods from porcelain to lightning conductors (essential because of the storms on the high plateau). He ran an experimental farm and built the monumental, wooden queen's palace at Antananarivo; it was later encased in stone by the Scots missionary Cameron, and still dominates the city today.

Laborde's locally produced goods meant that the country had even less need for foreign products. The queen therefore acted against the remaining traders operating in the coastal areas. By obliging foreign traders to submit to Malagasy law, and thus risk

18 View of Antananarivo about 1858, showing the Queen's Palace built by Jean Laborde and a procession of the royal family in the foreground

slavery, she forced them out. This led to a British and French bombardment of the east coast town of Tamatave in 1845, which again resulted in the ending of all foreign contacts.

Yet despite these breaks with the outside world and despite the persecution of the Christians, Ranavalona and her supporters were unable to prevent completely the invasion of foreign influences. Christianity had gone underground where, as so often elsewhere, it flourished, even reaching into the ranks of the ruling élite.

Apart from religion, the need to admit some foreigners who could maintain the supply of certain goods and undertake the trade monopolies of the ruling élite meant that the country was now dealing only with French adventurers. This was dangerous, as it was France that was most interested in Madagascar. Napoleon III, the new French emperor, was ready for foreign adventures and the Catholic church on Réunion was eager to replace the Malagasy Protestant church that had been set up by the London Missionary Society. The result was inevitable: conspiracy and eventual collision.

Although there is no evidence to support the rumours and legends that Jean Laborde was Queen Ranavalona's lover, it is true that he became Prince Rakoto's second 'father'. Under his influence the prince became the exact opposite of his mother: gentle, serious, religious and interested in the outside world, which inevitably meant France. He was also to fall under the influence of a French trader and shipowner called Lambert. He had been permitted to visit the capital in 1855 after one of his ships had relieved a starving Merina garrison on the coast that had been cut off by the ban on foreign ships. He came to Antananarivo with a Jesuit missionary disguised as his secretary and so the two-pronged French penetration began.

Lambert directed all his energies towards the prince and eventually persuaded him to sign the extraordinary Lambert Charter by which the Frenchman was given virtually all rights to exploit the resources of Madagascar. However it was obvious that so grotesque a document was meaningless as long as Ranavalona was queen. The next stage was a plot in 1857 to remove her. This might have succeeded had it not been for the arrival of the Reverend William Ellis, who was trying to persuade the queen to change her policy towards the English missionaries. There is no evidence that he told the queen of the plot, but it is more than likely that he found a way to let it be known. The queen reacted violently.

The Europeans, including Laborde, de Lastelle and Lambert, were expelled from the island. The already harsh punishments were accelerated with thousands being punished with slavery or mutilation. But to the sixty-nine-year-old queen her only son could do no wrong. She believed that he had been led astray and she preferred to blame others. This period of upheaval halted the island's development. The workers at Laborde's factory had been conscripted by the queen. They were not paid and did not like working in the factories. With their master gone they completely destroyed the industrial complex at Mantasoa. As her reign approached its end Queen Ranavalona I finally ruled over a nation almost free of foreign influence.

But we must not imagine that hers was a squalid, barbaric court. Even the disapproving missionary William Ellis felt able to describe the splendour of a state ball: the path up the hill to the palace was lined with her white-robed bodyguard; the queen, under a red silk umbrella and dressed in a green and purple flounced crinoline, received her guests in the courtyard before they went in to a banquet served on the finest imported porcelain. Or again where Ellis describes his first presentation at court:

The Queen and court were assembled in the upper verandah or balcony. Her majesty occupied the central place, her seat being raised above the rest, and covered with green damask. Her niece, the princess Rabodo, and the female members of the court, sat on her right hand; her son, next to her, on the left; then her nephew, the other members of her family, and the chief officers of the government. A large scarlet silk umbrella, embroidered and fringed with gold, was held or fixed over the queen, and a smaller scarlet umbrella, without ornament, was over the princess.

The queen's figure is not tall, but rather stout, her face round, the forehead well formed, the eyes small, the chin slightly rounded. The whole head and face small, compact, and well proportioned; her expression of countenance rather agreeable than otherwise, though at times indicating great firmness. She looked in good health, and vigorous, considering her age, which is said to be sixty-eight. Her majesty wore a crown made of plates of gold, with an ornament and charm, something like a gold crocodile's tooth, in the front plate; she had also a necklace and large earrings of gold. Her dress was a white satin lamba, with sprigs of gold, which, considering the lamba as the national Hova costume, was quite a queenly dress. The prince, her son, wore his star, and a coronet of apparently green velvet, bordered with a ring and band of leaves of massive silver. His cousin, Prince Ramboasalama, wore a black velvet cap embroidered with gold. Many of the officers wore silk lambas over their clothes.[2]

We must be grateful to Ellis for taking a camera with him. Engravings of his photographs have given us a unique record of the royal family. He became very friendly with Crown Prince Rakoto and the Crown Princess Rabodo and he invited them to the house where he was staying to have their photographs taken:

By daybreak the next morning I had commenced my preparations, and brought out my camera; and about seven o'clock the prince and princess

19   An audience at Queen Ranavalona's palace, Antananarivo, from William Ellis, *Three Visits to Madagascar*, 1858

came. I had not expected them so early. On this occasion, the covering of the princess's palanquin, fixed something like the hood of a chaise, was thrown back. The prince assisted her to step out, and then led her into the house to show her the apparatus and materials. I then invited the princess and her three female companions or attendants into my dwelling-house, while I prepared the chemicals. When I was ready, the princess, having changed her head-dress, came out into the courtyard. She wore an olive green silk dress, and had on her head a sort of cap composed of blue ribbons, with a gilt Maltese cross in front; small portions of her hair, very neatly braided in the Malagasy fashion, appearing about her temples on each side. She wore also a rich necklace of jewels, with earrings to match. I asked her to sit as much at ease as possible. Having exposed the plate nearly a minute, I then covered the lens, and told her it was finished. As I was taking it back to the house, the prince and princess asked if they might come in, and, accompanied by the officer from the palace, they entered and the princess could not restrain the expression of surprise and wonder, as the colourless plate became darkened, and the picture came out of itself more and more distinctly, after I had poured the transparent mixture out of the glass on to its surface.[3]

Many people, like Ellis, had high hopes that things would change when Rakoto came to the throne. Ranavalona now had only a few years left to live, years which by her own standards she spent peacefully.But she must have known that these were only years of waiting. She had held back the great river of European power but smaller streams had penetrated the dam. To some of the Merina, much later, during the 1930s when French colonialism was firmly established, she represented their greatest moment of independence. But her life and the results of her policies were so far-reaching that any judgement must be more complex than that. Although she was in some ways a figurehead for the principal male personalities of the Merina ruling class, no individual was allowed to dominate her court. There is no suggestion that her private world interfered with her political judgement; if her lover was her chief minister it was for the latter that he had been chosen. The only way she betrayed her policies was by permitting her mother-love to override the fact that Rakoto was totally opposed to all her aims.

Prince Rakoto came to the throne as King Radama II, a name that indicated his intention to continue with the work of his namesake, work interrupted by the reign of his mother. The exiled Frenchmen returned to Antananarivo and the process of political reversal began.

After Radama II, three more women came to the throne[4] until the eventual French conquest in 1896 ended the monarchy. All were mere puppets of the Andafiavaratra family—Ranavalona I was the first and last woman to rule as well as reign over the 'Great Island'.

20   Prince Rakoto and Princess Rabodo, from William Ellis, *Three Visits to Madagascar*, 1858

NOTES

1 Called Tananarive by the French, the Malagasy now wish the name of their capital to revert to its more exact spelling.
2 William Ellis, *Three Visits to Madagascar* (London: John Murray, 1858), pp. 380–1.
3 Ibid., p. 412.
4 Queen Rasoherina (reigned 1863–8) and Queen Ranavalona II (reigned 1868–83), wives of Radama II; Queen Ranavalona III (reigned 1883–96; d. 1917), great niece of Ranavalona II, exiled to Algiers in 1897 following the French invasion.

FURTHER READING

Mervyn Brown, *Madagascar Rediscovered* (London: Damien Tunnacliffe, 1978).
William Ellis, *Three Visits to Madagascar* (London: John Murray, 1858).
Nigel Heseltine, *Madagascar* (London: Pall Mall Press, 1971).

10
Muganzirwazza of Buganda

ABOUT 1817–82

Of the four great kingdoms in what is today Uganda—Bunyoro, Ankole, Buganda and Busoga—the cattle-raising Bunyoro were at first the leading group. But by the last century when the first visitors left us written records it was the farming Baganda whose power the others feared.

Despite their rivalry the Bunyoro and Baganda had many things in common, particularly in the way they chose their kings. Each clan sent a wife to the king and from among the male children a new king was chosen who belonged to his mother's clan and would one day be buried on their land. So by this 'chance' method no king's clan was set up; all the clans were equal for the new king would in turn take a wife from each clan, any one of which might produce the next king.

Among the Baganda it was the *kabaka*'s mother, the *namasole*, who came second in the system of government, after her was the *katikiro*, the prime minister. She had control of the royal women as well as her own chiefs and lands. If the new *kabaka* was still young she would rule on his behalf; if he died young she would be a member of the council who chose the next king.

The strength of the Baganda lay in their efficient system of fighting. Their main farming crop was the *matoke* banana or plantain, which the women cultivated leaving the men free for war or public service. In this way a strong centralized state was set up ruled from a vast wooden city set on a hill. At the centre of this city was the Lubiri, the *kabaka*'s palace. Inside were his audience compound, the scores of thatched huts for the many wives and their servants, the kitchens and store rooms. There were quarters for the hundreds of royal pages sent by the clans in the hope that they would be promoted to one of the positions of influence within the kingdom.

The Namasole Muganzirwazza

Kabaka Suna II had 148 wives, an indication of the expansion of the kingdom and of the king's need to extend his power by marriage over new territories and subjects. After Suna's death in about 1856 there was much discussion among the senior court officials as to his successor. The problem was to find a candidate who would not feel the need to avenge past actions by the court officials. It was perhaps for this reason that out of the sixty-one eligible sons they chose one of the younger princes, the son of Muganzirwazza, who already exercised considerable influence in the kingdom. The boy, Mukaabaya, became Kabaka Mutesa I, one of the most famous rulers in African history.

We know so much about this period because of the rich oral tradition that has come down to us and because eight years after Mutesa came to the throne the English explorer John Hanning Speke came to Buganda on his journey to find the source of the Nile. But by the time of his visit in 1862 Muganzirwazza's authority was already waning. She had at first dominated her quiet, rather inno-cent-looking son, but gradually he began to prove himself a capable if violent man. Mutesa's unexpected punishments and his frequent use of the death penalty made him the undisputed and much feared ruler of his people. By the time of Speke's arrival the Baganda kingdom was changing from a group of chiefs loosely led by the *kabaka* to a situation where the all-powerful king ruled alone through his appointed officials.

The arrival of Arab slave traders bringing guns gave Mutesa the wealth and the weapons he needed to ensure his supremacy. Muganzirwazza was gradually forced to retire from the centre of power.

Speke had passed through the kingdom of Karagwe on his way to Buganda. There he and his companion James Grant had been graciously received by the king, Rumanika. But Speke was keen to get to Buganda and so on to the source of the White Nile. Grant had an ulcerated knee and was left behind while Speke set off for the Buganda capital.

The Englishman was amazed by the vast city of thatched huts when he arrived at its entrance on 19 February 1862. He was taken to see the *kabaka* the following day and presented the excited young Mutesa with the gifts he had brought from England. A week after his arrival Mutesa informed Speke that it was customary for visitors to go and see the queen mother, a sign that although her influence was waning she still ranked second after her son. Speke's record of the visit is one of the most famous and often retold scenes in the story of Africa's encounter with Europe:

The palace to be visited lay half a mile beyond the king's, but the highroad to it was forbidden me, as it is considered uncourteous to pass the king's gate without going in. So after winding through back-gardens, the slums of Bandowaroga, I struck upon the highroad close to her majesty's where everything looked like the royal palace on a miniature scale. A large cleared space divided the queen's residence from her Kamraviona's [her chief official or courtier]. The outer enclosures and courts were fenced with tiger-grass; and the huts, though neither so numerous nor so large, were constructed after the same fashion as the king's. Guards also kept the doors, on which large bells were hung to give alarm, and officers in waiting watched the thronerooms. All the huts were full of women, save those kept as waiting-rooms, where drums and harmonicons were placed for amusement. On first entering, I was required to sit in a waiting-hut till my arrival was announced; but that did not take long, as the queen was prepared to receive me; and being of a more affable disposition than her son, she held rather a levée of amusement than a stiff court of show. I entered the throne-hut as the gate of that court was thrown open, with my hat off, but umbrella held over my head, and walked straight towards her till ordered to sit upon my bundle of grass. [1]

Muganzirwazza was—according to Speke—'fat, fair and forty-five', dressed simply in an excellent fine bark-cloth for which the Baganda are renowned. She was as fascinated by the white man as he was by her and wanted to enjoy his visit. *Pombe*, the East African spirit, was served and pipes were smoked while musicians played and danced.

21   Speke introduces Grant to Muganzirwazza, from Speke's *Journal*, 1863

Muganzirwazza seems to have had a sense of fun and decided to flirt with the stranger. Having gone off to change her dress for a different-coloured robe she returned and took up three sticks. 'This stick', she said, 'represents my stomach, which gives me much uneasiness; this second stick my liver, which causes shooting pains all over my body; and the third one my heart, for I get constant dreams at night about Sunna, my late husband, and they are not pleasant.' Happily, Speke was not a typical Victorian 'gentleman'; he had enough sense of humour to enjoy the situation.

The dreams and sleeplessness I told her was a common widow's complaint, and could only be cured by her majesty making up her mind to marry a second time; but before I could advise for the bodily complaints, it would be necessary for me to see her tongue, feel her pulse, and perhaps also, her sides. Hearing this, the Wakungu said, 'Oh, that can never be allowed without the sanction of the King;' but the queen, rising to her feet, expressed her scorn at the idea of taking advice from a mere stripling, and submitted herself for examination.

Having examined her he gave her some medicine and advised her not to drink *pombe* for a while. He then presented the customary gifts and prepared to leave. 'Still she said I had not yet satisfied her; I must return again two days hence for she liked me much—excessively—she could not say how much; but now the day was gone, I might go.'

Despite this excellent beginning the next meetings were to prove frustrating. The explorer was often kept waiting or made to spend long days drinking and listening to music. The problem was that to the Baganda he was only a curiosity. In order to get the assistance he needed to carry on with his expedition he tried to play off the *kabaka* against his mother by making each jealous of his attentions to the other. He would teach the *kabaka* to shoot one day and flirt with his mother the next. What comes through his records of these meetings is that Muganzirwazza paid him no attention except during her moments of relaxation. Despite the decline in her power she was still the powerful superior of several of the clan chiefs. She had her territories and officials to administer and this is what she would have been doing while Speke waited outside her compound. Unfortunately for us he was not allowed to see her at work and his record of her shows only a carefree widow trying to enjoy herself.

Nevertheless, Speke successfully befriended both son and mother. In fact she presented him with two young serving girls. We are lucky that Speke was not the prude that so many of his fellow-Victorian travellers pretended to be—he seems to have thoroughly enjoyed the company of the Baganda women. One day when the *kabaka*'s shooting party came to a river Speke carried the girls across on his back; on another having been approached by Kariana, the wife of one of the *kabaka*'s ministers, he offered her his arm and walked along, 'as if we had been in Hyde Park rather than in Central Africa, flirting and coqueting all the way'.

Thanks to the influence of the queen mother, Speke became very friendly with Mutesa. But then he began to visit Muganzirwazza less frequently, which made her complain.

Eventually Grant was able to make the journey to Buganda and was presented to the queen mother. She seems to have been more respectable and subdued with Grant, who was the quieter of the two white men. Grant was to describe Muganzirwazza as a pleasant, homely woman, hardly the same person who had flirted with his companion!

Mutesa eventually permitted the two explorers to continue their journey, though he chose an unpleasant way to show his anger and grief at their departure:

> *On the way home, one of the king's favourite women overtook us, taken with her hands clasped at the back of her head, to execution crying, 'N'yawo!' in the most pitiful manner. A man was preceding her, but did not touch her; for she loved to obey the orders of her king voluntarily, and, in consequence of previous attachment, was permitted, as a mark of distinction, to walk free. Wondrous world! it was not ten minutes since we parted from the king, yet he had found time to transact this bloody piece of business.*

22   One of the king's wives being taken to execution, from Speke's *Journal*, 1863

Results of the visit

So Speke and Grant passed on but not quite out of Buganda's history. Eventually Mutesa was to centralize power completely in his own hands. His sister Nassuna was the only woman who was able to influence him. Despite being always surrounded by his officials and his wives, Mutesa no doubt felt lonely. Only someone of high rank like Nassuna could understand him and so he spent much time just chatting with her. This isolation continued by successive *kabakas* was to prove their undoing; for when the various foreigners, Arabs and Europeans, who were coming to Buganda in increasing numbers, began to spread their respective religions among the clans, it was the king who remained apart and in opposition to them. Unable to give up their wives because that would weaken their authority, the *kabakas* could not be baptized and were eventually at odds with the new converts to Christianity. The persecution of Christians (the 'Ugandan Martyrs') by Mutesa's son, Mwanga II, led to his expulsion in 1888 and resulted in the curbing of the *kabaka's* authority.

Yet despite Muganzirwazza's limited role during Speke's visit, their friendship was to have a lasting effect over her people's future. His largely favourable reports of the power and stability of the Buganda kingdom led to the British giving it special status within the protectorate they established in 1894 over the territory, which then became Uganda. This status has echoes even today in the uneasy position of the Baganda within the modern republic of Uganda, a position that has led to much of the trouble of recent years.

For John Hanning Speke, his relations with Muganzirwazza were to have unfortunate consequences. His account of his stay in Buganda led to accusations of immorality from his Victorian critics; his claims to have proved that Lake Victoria was the source of the White Nile were also disputed. He shot himself in 1864, though whether by accident or design is not proven.

Muganzirwazza outlived him by eighteen years, dying in 1882. Despite having successfully stripped her of her powers, Mutesa was distressed at her death. He accused Sekibobo, his commander-in-chief, of killing her by witchcraft and would have put him to death but for the intervention of one of the visiting missionaries. Mutesa asked the white men how queens were buried in England and was told that three coffins were used, one being of lead to preserve the body, and that is how her funeral was arranged. That the cruel Mutesa should have grieved for someone, even though it was his mother, says much for Muganzirwazza, the last of the powerful queen mothers of the East African kingdoms.

NOTES

[1] All the quotations in this chapter are taken from J. H. Speke, *Journal of the Journey to find the Source of the Nile* (London: William Blackwood and Sons, 1863), pp. 304–450.

FURTHER READING

Apolo Kaggwa, (trans. Kiwanuka), *The Kings of Buganda* (Nairobi: East African Publishing House, 1971).

M.S.M.S. Kiwanuka, *History of Buganda* (London: Longman, 1971).

Alexander Maitland, *Speke* (London: Constable, 1971).

J. H. Speke, *Journal of the Journey to find the Source of the Nile* (London: William Blackwood and Sons, 1863).

11
Yaa Asantewa of Asante

ABOUT 1840/60–1921

In their attempts to subdue the various lands that were to make up their West African empire, the British found few people as difficult as the Asante of Ghana. For nearly a hundred years, first British traders, later the British government, attempted to break the power of Asante. Yet even in the end, when they were so weakened that a British victory seemed certain, the Asante still held back an army equipped with deadly modern weapons for a short final period of independence. When all seemed lost, their power broken and their king exiled, the Asante put themselves under the command of a woman, Queen Yaa Asantewa, who led them in their last desperate attempt to keep the foreigners at bay. To understand why they did this it is necessary to understand the importance of the Golden Stool to the Asante nation and to appreciate the role that royal women have played in its history.

Osei Tutu, the first *asantehene* (or ruler) of all the Asante, had united the Akan states in the 1670s, rallying them against the overlordship of the neighbouring Denkyira. Osei Tutu wanted to unite his new nation and so with the assistance of a friend and priest, Okomfo Anokye, created a national faith, the story of the Golden Stool. This tells how, at a great gathering in Kumasi, the new capital, a wooden stool ornamented with gold appeared out of a cloud of dust amid lightning and thunder and floated gently down on to Osei Tutu's knees. All paid homage to the stool which was accepted as the unifying symbol of the Asante. Although the rulers succeeding Osei Tutu are said to be 'on the stool' when reigning, this is merely a figure of speech, for no one ever *sat* on the Golden Stool: it was considered to be greater than the *asantehene* himself and on ceremonial occasions was set higher than him on a throne of its own.

By conquering their overlords, the Denkyira, the Asante under Osei Tutu trebled both their land and population. After a brief period of civil war the second great *asantehene* Opoku Ware (d. 1750) created the Asante empire by the conquest of their neighbours, while the seventh *asantehene* Osei Bonsu (*c.* 1779–1824)

carried the conquest to the sea by defeating in 1806–7 some of the
Fante states that controlled the flow of European goods from the
coast to Kumasi. Further coastal wars in 1811 and 1816 brought the
Asante into conflict with the British. They were at first successful,
but the Asante imperial system had a fatal flaw: the conquered states
were never fully assimilated nor their armies dispersed and this
independence left them ever ready to revolt when circumstances
permitted. After the first encounter the British traders on the coast
feared the Asante. The policy of the main group of British traders,
the African Company of Merchants, was to side with the coastal
peoples near to their forts. This placed the traders in opposition to
what the Asante considered to be their concerns within *their* empire.
Later the British government sent officials who replaced the officers
of the Company as British representatives on the coast, but this
policy was not changed. (For map see p. 23.)

After Osei Bonsu's occupation of southern Fante territory in 1807
trade between Asante and the coast declined. The British attempted
to outlaw the slave trade from which the Asante profited. Fighting
broke out in the 1820s with a further Asante success in 1824. It was
the last. The British were becoming better established on the coast
and the Asante decided to make peace in 1831. It was an uneasy

23   The Golden Stool and Asantehene Prempeh II. The Golden
Stool occupies its own chair of state. This picture was taken in
the 1930s.

peace, but one that lasted for thirty years until the Asante again attempted to challenge the British position. The result was the invasion of 1874 when a British expeditionary force under Sir Garnet Wolseley reached Kumasi and shattered Asante confidence in their army.

Britain now established the Gold Coast colony on the coast. Asantehene Kofi Karikari was deposed by his people and his successor Mensa Bonsu attempted to re-establish a strong empire. But the Asante were divided among themselves and in 1883 Mensa Bonsu was himself deposed. The situation worsened when his successor Kwaku Dua II died of smallpox in 1884, the year that he was enstooled.

It is now that we begin to find mention of a woman who was later to become the most important female leader in Asante history. The importance of women in Asante government is shown by the fact that a new *asantehene* was selected by the queen mother, in consultation with certain advisers, from among her daughter's sons or her daughter's daughter's sons. From earliest times, in the different Akan states, the queen mother had ruled when the king died or was deposed and no successor had been appointed. There are legends of women rulers leading their warriors into battle, but even these legends are hardly as exciting as the true story of Yaa Asantewa the queen mother of Edweso (Ejisu).

Edweso is one of the Asante states, about 16 kilometres east of Kumasi. In 1884 its ruler (the *edwesohene*) was Nana Afrane Kuma and his main adviser was his mother, Queen Yaa Asantewa. She had been born in Edweso sometime between 1840 and 1860 and she may have been forty years old when she was enstooled as queen mother. She was a formidable-looking woman: 'A thin, brown, leathery old lady, with fierce blazing eyes', as one of her later British enemies was to describe her.[1] She might have lived out her life as nothing more than an important local figure in Edweso had it not been for the upheaval that followed Kwaku Dua II's death in 1884.

The disputes surrounding the attempt to inherit the empire by Kwaku Dua's brother Prempeh I were so fierce that they began Asante's disintegration. Civil war broke out and the various Asante states took sides. Yaa Asantewa was a member of the same Oyoko clan as Prempeh I and she and her son Nana Afrane Kuma remained loyal to the new *asantehene*.

It was ten years before Prempeh I could be formally enstooled and during those years the British plotted in the rebellious states, signing treaties and offering them protection against Prempeh.

In 1894, the same year as Prempeh's enstoolment, the British tried to send a Resident, or representative of their government, to live in Kumasi. Prempeh's refusal led to the British expedition of 1896 and he was forced to agree. He accepted a British protectorate, but when he claimed that he could not pay the money that the expedition cost he was arrested with some of his courtiers and exiled to the Seychelles Islands. Exiled with him was Yaa Asantewa's son Nana Afrane Kuma, a fact that was to have far-reaching consequences for the unsuspecting conquerors.

It seemed to the British that Asante power had disintegrated and for the next four years nothing prevented the establishment of the British Residency in Kumasi and the construction of a fort to house the small but growing administration. It was true that many of the Asante states and most of the once-conquered territories may not have been sorry to see the power of the *asantehene* broken. But the peoples around Kumasi recognized Prempeh as their local lord, not merely as their overlord and there was immediate and vigorous opposition to the British. That the hidden meetings and secret military preparations centred on a woman was not, as we have seen, unusual in Akan society. The senior woman, the queen mother, was not only paramount in women's affairs but had a distinct voice in all public affairs: indeed, when Prempeh I was exiled his mother was sent with him. R. S. Baden-Powell, the founder of the Boy Scout movement, who was a major at the time of the British expedition to Kumasi, witnessed the humiliating ceremony when Prempeh was forced to submit himself to the British governor. He later noted that: 'The only "man" among them was the Queen.'[2]

Certainly the queen mother of all-Asante could have encouraged the simmering rebellion had she not been exiled. That this position

24   The British fort at Kumasi in 1900

of leadership now fell to Yaa Asantewa and not to another can only be because she had made herself the most eligible candidate. She hated the British for their shabby treatment of Prempeh and her son and during the four years after the establishment of the British Residency in Kumasi she built up Asante hatred for the strangers in their midst.

She cannot have expected that the British would play so completely into her hands. The governor of the Gold Coast, Sir Frederick Hodgson, decided to pay his first official visit to Kumasi on 25 March 1900, accompanied by his wife and other prominent British officials. Seldom has a colonial officer blundered quite so badly as Sir Frederick did on 28 March 1900. During the course of the 'celebrations' he received the Asante nobility and addressed a few 'chosen' words to them. His Excellency's private secretary later described the presentations: 'The old Queen-Mother of Ejissu [Edweso], Queen Ashantuah, whose name has since figured so largely in the rebellion, caused much amusement by carefully examining the Governor's medals.'[3]

She was no doubt weighing up a trinket that she would have liked to get her hands on, a possibility brought nearer by the governor's speech a short time later. He complained that the money for the expedition remained unpaid. Then he went on to ask where the Golden Stool was and why it had not been surrendered. It must, he continued, be brought out so that he, the representative of the British Queen, might sit upon it. Only someone ignorant of the nature of the stool could have suggested such a sacrilege. The meeting ended in silence, a deceptive silence, for all the listeners went off to prepare to defend their national honour. That night the chiefs met and made their plans. Three days later the Yaa Asantewa war began, named for the woman who inspired it.

The governor had sent a detachment of men to try to find the Golden Stool. On their return empty-handed they reported the unrest in the surrounding countryside. Sir Frederick at last recognized the true danger of his position and tried to negotiate. But the Asante insisted on the return of Prempeh, something that the governor was unable to promise. He telegraphed urgently to the coast for help, but when the telegraph wire was cut his situation became more desperate. By 25 April Kumasi was surrounded and the British and those they 'protected' were trapped in the fort, short of food and ammunition. They were to remain there for two months.

They received little help from those states that had not actively joined Yaa Asantewa's war. Even their principal ally, the king of Bekwai, was not only terrified to send warriors to relieve Kumasi in case Yaa Asantewa invaded his territory, but he was also barely able to stop his own men from joining her.

By mid-June thirty people a day were dying in the fort and the British decided to attempt to break out. On 23 June the escape was made, leaving 153 men to hold the fort. Despite small attacks, the Asante made little attempt to prevent them escaping, which they could have done had they wished. After suffering great hardship on the journey the small and exhausted party arrived back at Cape Coast, seventeen days later.

In the meantime the British had rushed 1,400 troops from other parts of Africa and sent them to relieve the Kumasi garrison and to suppress the Asante who now numbered between 40,000 and 50,000. The British troops relieved the fort on 15 July and then set about wiping out the stockades that had been built all round Kumasi as centres of resistance. Eyewitness accounts frequently emphasize the bravery of the Asante whenever faced with the enemy. Given her age it is unlikely that Yaa Asantewa actively led her troops. The military organization was mainly under the command of one of her chiefs, Kofi Kofia, though there is a photograph said to be of Yaa Asantewa, dressed for battle and holding a rifle.

On all occasions the Asante fought on to the end, outmatched by the new weapons with which the relief force was armed. Despite this superiority it took the British over three months before they began to break the resistance. On 29 August, 350 men, some armed with Maxim guns, set off for Edweso to capture Yaa Asantewa. Her stockade was defended by 3,000 men who were blasted by the British guns. Despite this, the survivors retreated rather than sub-mit. But as the end of September approached only a handful of chiefs along with the queen mother were still at liberty. She sent envoys to see what terms her enemies required, but they were so roughly treated and insulted by some of the enemy African soldiers that they returned. The angry old queen determined to fight on.

The battle began on 30 September when 1,200 men from various British African regiments finally succeeded in wearing down the last major Asante group, beating them into bloody defeat and rout. Yaa Asantewa evaded capture and was able to avoid her pursuers for a short while longer. Eventually she and her last remaining chiefs were captured when the Ahafu forest where she was hiding was surrounded by troops. Her chiefs were captured, Yaa Asantewa last of all. The British officer who arrested her claimed that she spat in his face.[4] In the end it had taken nearly 2,000 troops to capture her.

There were a few executions, but the 'rebellion' had made the British more cautious in dealing with the Asante. Most of the cap-tured chiefs were treated as prisoners of war. Yaa Asantewa was

25   Yaa Asantewa (right) may have posed in this way for the camera, rather than for actual combat

exiled to the Seychelles where she had the consolation of joining her son. She lived for another twenty or so years, dying after a short illness, probably in 1921. It must have been a sad exile for so active a woman and a hard separation from the land to which she was devoted. She is unlikely to have had much news of events in Asante and would not have had the satisfaction of knowing that, following her uprising, her people were to be treated with a far greater respect than they had been on that fateful day when Governor Hodgson thought he should sit upon the Golden Stool. A few years after her death Prempeh I was brought back from exile and in 1935 his son Prempeh II was restored as *asantehene*: a recognition by the colonial power that the people they had sought to divide were remarkably united after all, a unity that Yaa Asantewa had done much to preserve. The Asante still sing of her: 'Yaa Asantewa, the warrior woman who carries a gun and a sword of state in battle'.

NOTES
[1] Heard on a radio broadcast, 2 November 1937, by W. M. Hall and recounted in his *The Great Drama of Kumasi* (London: Putnam, 1939).
[2] Major R. S. Baden-Powell, *The Downfall of Prempeh* (London: Methuen and Co., 1898), p. 126.
[3] Captain Sir Cyril Armitage (Private Secretary to Sir Frederick Hodgson, Governor of the Gold Coast).
[4] Quoted in W. M. Hall, op. cit., p. 9.

FURTHER READING
William Tordoff, *Asanti Under the Prempehs 1888–1935* (London: Oxford University Press, 1965).
Major Frederick Myatt, *The Golden Stool, An account of the Asanti War of 1900* (London: William Kimber, 1966).
Ivor Wilks, *Asante in the Nineteenth Century* (Cambridge: Cambridge University Press, 1975).

12
Nehanda of Zimbabwe

ABOUT 1863–98

The struggle for the liberation of Zimbabwe has a long history stretching back to the last century when large numbers of white people entered the country and occupied the land. Many women and girls took part in the final war of independence that led to majority rule in 1980. They could draw inspiration from the fact that one of the major leaders of the first resistance to white rule was a woman—Nehanda[1].

Today the women of Zimbabwe have won their fight but in the last century Nehanda was to suffer and die for her courage. Like Dona Beatrice (see Chapter 7) she was a spiritual leader forced by circumstances to direct her people's resistance to foreign influences. Like the Kahina (see Chapter 3) she was a prophet, a medium who was able when possessed by the spirit of the original Nehanda to guide those who came to her for advice.

There is a tradition that the original Nehanda lived sometime in the fifteenth century and was the daughter of a chief of the northern Shona. Today there are many stories about that time. One myth is that when the chief died, one of his sons had to establish his authority as in Ancient Egypt by committing incest with his sister. Legend states that when Nehanda's father died, only one of her brothers was willing to perform this rite. Afterwards Nehanda was so dismayed that she disappeared into a cleft in a rocky hill which to this day is called Gumbi re Nehanda. Although the original Nehanda disappeared, her spirit returns as a guardian of her people.[2]

Nehanda became one of the most important of the Lion spirits of the Shona, so called because after the death of one medium, the spirit wanders the bush in the form of a lion until a new medium is found. The new medium is only aware that she has been chosen when long periods of illness begin and when, in a trance, she begins to speak the messages of Nehanda. When this happens, other mediums of other Lion spirits come to examine the sick woman to be sure that this is truly the new Nehanda.

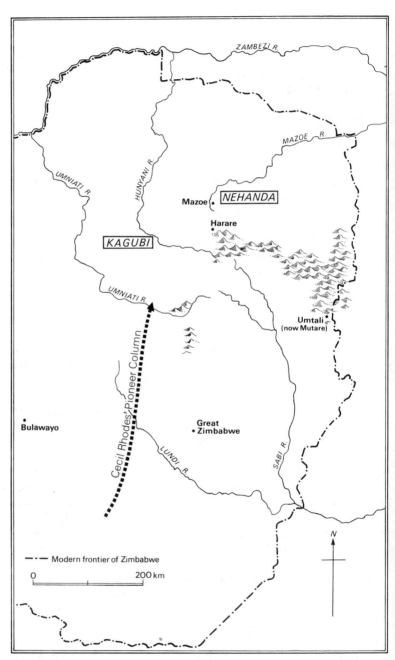

Zimbabwe in the 1890s

At the time of the white invasions which began in 1890, the Nehanda medium was a woman originally called Chargwe. She was born sometime around 1863 and in a photograph taken in her mid-thirties she appears as a small, plump woman with stern features. When possessed by the spirit, she lived in the traditional shrine of the Nehanda in the Mazoe valley. Exactly when she became possessed is not known, but she was already established and influential when the missionaries and traders began to arrive in the Mazoe area after Cecil Rhodes' Pioneer Column had run up its flag on Harare Hill in 1890. At her shrine the Nehanda medium would advise those who came to consult her and would perform the traditional ceremonies that ensured rain and good crops. It was because of these functions that the white invaders called her a witch and thought of her as something evil, someone of whom their God would not approve. What they did not understand was that the Lion spirits were not witches or rain-gods in the eyes of the Shona. The Shona believed in one God whom they called Mwari and the Lion spirits were only there to help the people understand Mwari's wishes. In fact, when the first Christian missionaries came to Mazoe, the Nehanda medium thought that they too were teaching the people about Mwari and she advised everyone to cooperate with them. As a result of Nehanda's influence, the missionaries and other white visitors to Mazoe were treated with friendship and respect; unfortunately they did not reciprocate.

The British adventurer Cecil Rhodes and other white leaders thought that they would find little resistance to their attempt to move north from South Africa in search of new farming lands and gold mines. They even put forward a moral reason for an invasion: they would put an end to fighting between the country's two main peoples, the Ndebele and the Shona. It was true that the Ndebele had driven out the Shona from the south-west and established their own kingdom when they entered these lands in the middle of the nineteenth century. But in a major battle in 1885 the Shona had proved that they could defend themselves and the two groups had accepted that each would have part of the country. Relations between the two were far from being those of master and slave as the white man imagined. There was mutual respect and many points of contact between them, not least because the Ndebele adopted most of the Shona religious beliefs in order to be 'at peace with the land' they had conquered.

Throughout the 1880s various European adventurers, often with the backing of their governments, had used every means of treachery to weaken the Ndebele king, Lobengula. By the end of his reign, the British, in the person of Cecil Rhodes, were Lobengula's main problem. The Shona did not have a central government which meant that they were more easily overrun by Rhodes's British South

Africa Company in 1890. It took a further three years before the Ndebele were finally defeated and Lobengula fled.

At first there was an uneasy calm as the people absorbed what had happened, but the aftermath of the invasion was disastrous. It soon appeared that the conquerors had not 'made peace with the land'. Cattle died, crops failed and violence threatened.

When Nehanda heard that the Europeans were in the Mazoe area she said to the chiefs, 'Don't be afraid of them—they are only traders. But take a black cow to them and say: this is the meat with which we greet you.'[3]

These early arrivals were looking for gold which was easily found in river beds or near the surface of the ground. Traditionally it had been extracted by women. With Nehanda's cooperation, trade in gold was established but such friendly gestures were not to last. The white leaders soon began to establish their rule. Forced labour was recruited and taxes imposed. Worse still was the arrogance and cruelty of these new self-appointed masters. Anyone could be beaten at will and many were. Even for a minor offence a man might be tied by the neck to a forked post and flogged till he bled. One of the cruellest of the new overlords was the Native Commissioner for Nehanda's area, a man called Pollard whose indiscriminate floggings were a major source of discontent.

The various mediums around the country were in constant communication with each other by secret messengers. Presents were exchanged, news circulated and plans prepared. Travelling by night, messengers passed between Nehanda and the other leading Shona Lion spirit, a man called Kagubi. Nehanda and Kagubi agreed that action would have to be taken. As a song of the time put it, 'the white cobra must be killed'.[4] Nehanda and Kagubi spread the word that the white man would be hunted down like game. When news came that the Ndebele were openly in revolt, the two Shona mediums sent orders for their people to join the rising.

The Ndebele revolt began in 1896. Cecil Rhodes had not expected the Shona to take part as well because he considered them docile and cowardly. They did, however, and the Europeans were nearly driven from the land.

It began with the capture of the hated Pollard. He was brought to Nehanda and was made to work as her servant for a time. Later he was executed. Then Nehanda ordered her people to go and rid the country of the invaders. She made it clear that they were not to touch anything that belonged to the enemy. She knew that if the uprising became a greedy search for loot, the white men would easily win. From June to August 1896 the northern Shona were able to regain control of most of their lands.

Cecil Rhodes could not fight on so many fronts at the same time and after two months, decided to negotiate a settlement with the

Ndebele. But he was determined to crush the Shona. Until August 1896 the whites were forced to defend themselves under siege in their settlements while the rest of the land returned to traditional rule. Messages were passed by signal fires, uniting the chiefs, and for a time it seemed as if Shona government had been restored. Throughout this period Nehanda continued to encourage her people's resistance and to warn against any lowering of vigilance. But by the end of July the balance was tipped in favour of the British. An imperial force landed at Portuguese Beira and was despatched overland to Mutare (formerly Umtali). Then it marched on Harare (formerly Salisbury). Faced with this army equipped with deadly Maxim guns, the Shona uprising seemed doomed. Yet astonishingly, resistance was to continue until the end of 1897. For twelve violent months the imperial forces burned villages and crops and carried out deadly reprisals for what they saw as Shona treachery. Nehanda and Kagubi were still able to keep up the mood of resistance. Many of the villagers took refuge in neighbouring caves. Then the British discovered a way to force the Shona into submission. Sticks of dynamite were dropped through air holes into the caves causing appalling bloodshed below. Even the newspapers in Britain, which were usually stony-hearted, were obliged to protest at these horribly inhuman acts but still they continued.

In September 1897 one of the main Shona leaders, Chief Makoni, was lured out of his refuge. He had offered to surrender but he was hastily tried and shot. In October Kagubi himself surrendered, but Nehanda still struggled on. Having heard about the dynamiting of the caves, she decided to evacuate her own rocky sanctuary in Mazoe and head for the birthplace of the original Nehanda at Dande. Despite a large European force pursuing her, she managed to avoid them until December but it became clear to her that her followers would be killed if she was finally trapped. Nehanda therefore let herself be taken rather than cause any further deaths amongst her people. She was taken to Harare jail to await trial with Kagubi.

The trial was a foregone conclusion. It opened on 2 March 1898 with Kagubi accused of killing an African policeman and Nehanda of murdering Pollard. They were both found guilty and sentenced to be executed by hanging on 27 April. Up to the time of the execution, attempts were made by Father Richartz, a priest at the Chishawasha mission, to convert the prisoners to Christianity. Kagubi was eventually baptized. Nehanda proudly refused, dancing, laughing and talking until the warders were forced to tie her hands. As she was led to the scaffold to be hung, Nehanda continued to cry out her fierce resistance. She demanded to be sent back to her own people and continued to shout her message until the trap-door opened and she fell to her death.

26   The mediums Nehanda and Kagubi awaiting trial in 1897

The uprising had been defeated but 450 whites had been killed, one tenth of the total white population. The Shona for their part would never forget the courage of Nehanda and the tradition of a Nehanda medium continued. In 1906 the Native Commissioner for the Mazoe area received a report that a new Nehanda medium had been found. Many years later, in 1972, an old lady in her mid-eighties who was possessed by the Nehanda spirit, was taken from her home to a safe place across the Zambezi River by ZANLA guerrillas fighting against the white Rhodesians. The guerrillas consulted her about where to hide arms, what routes to take and where to fight. They called the northern area of fighting 'the Nehanda Sector'. This medium died on 12 June 1973 and independence came in April 1980. One day her remains will be taken back to her home in Zimbabwe for burial. Who can deny that at last Nehanda had her victory?

NOTES

[1] Sometimes spelt Nyanda.
[2] As with most legends, there are variations on this theme and different groups accept other stories. There have also been instances of more than one Nehanda medium at the same time but we are concerned here only with the central legend and the direct antecedents of the late nineteenth century Nehanda medium of the Mazoe area, as far as these can be deduced.
[3] Quoted by C. G. Chivanda in 'The Mashona Rebellion in Oral Tradition, Mazoe District', University College of Rhodesia, History Honours iii, Seminar Paper No. 9 (23 June 1966).
[4] Ibid.

FURTHER READING

T. O. Ranger, *Revolt in Southern Rhodesia 1896–7* (London: Heinemann, 1967).
David Martin and Phyllis Johnson, *The Struggle for Zimbabwe* (London: Faber, 1981; Harare: Zimbabwe Publishing House, 1982).

Index